ESKIMO CHILDHOOD AND INTERPERSONAL RELATIONSHIPS

Nunivak Biographies and Genealogies

MONOGRAPH 33

THE AMERICAN ETHNOLOGICAL SOCIETY, VERNE F. RAY, EDITOR

Eskimo Childhood and Interpersonal Relationships

NUNIVAK BIOGRAPHIES AND GENEALOGIES

By Margaret Lantis

UNIVERSITY OF WASHINGTON PRESS

SEATTLE AND LONDON

Genealogies and illustrations drawn by Edward G. Schumacher
Photographs by the author

Copyright © 1960 by the University of Washington Press
Second printing, 1972
Library of Congress Catalog Card Number: 60-16656
ISBN 0-295-74084-1
Printed in the United States of America

INTRODUCTION

At the beginning of World War II I spent (a chance coincidence) a year on Nunivak Island in east Bering Sea, providing me with a ground plan of its culture and a body of mythology. During the war, these data were written up and accepted for publication. As soon as possible after the war, the island was revisited for four months especially to collect materials for a study of personality, but also to study cultural changes and the current economy after several basic changes. These included the introduction of a reindeer slaughterhouse, shift of village store from private to community ownership and management, and partial shift from ceremonial house to government school as community center. Movies were taken of children at work and play, church and school records were scanned for family data, and other techniques were used, but the principal effort was put on Rorschach Tests, children's free drawings and Mosaic Block Tests, and personal histories.

In the study of childhood and youth, there were implicit hypotheses although none was stated. For example, because of extended kinship responsibility and cultural homogeneity, a child from a broken Nunivak family placed in a foster home would not suffer as much personality damage as in urban American culture. Because no projective tests had been tried in this locality, the principal objectives were (1) an experimental use of several techniques in personality study and the start of a long-term collection of clinical materials; (2) collection of additional materials (besides those obtained in 1939-40) for a study of the culture in operation, especially its social organization. Did it work in actuality as the Nunivakers said it did in principle? Some of the principles stated had been derived by the author from genealogies and other case material; but some generalizations, especially pertaining to the old religion, had been submitted by Nunivakers without adequate opportunity for testing.

This second reason for recording the personal histories is my principal reason for presenting them here. They are fragmentary compared with the book-length biographies obtained from a few Indians of the United States but they do show the personal aspects of those customs that anthropologists usually describe so impersonally, e.g., marriage, adoption, the making of a hunter, and the child's instruction in religion and social relationships. We see in the reminiscences of several people, probably better than in one long autobiography, the variance in culture, even in a small isolated group. Also, it is hoped, we see not "the Nunivak Eskimos" but individuals.

Time. Although the biographies were recorded in 1946 and their sequels recorded during a visit of a few weeks in the winter of 1955-56, contact with the Nunivakers has been frequent, almost continuous from 1946 to the present. We have corresponded; Nunivak patients in Alaska or Washington hospitals have been visited; and news has been obtained from mutual acquaintances. Whereas in 1939-40 Nunivak was about fifty years behind Nome, Unalakleet, or Bethel in acculturation—every winter and spring it would go four months without mail—today it is visited as frequently as villages on the neighboring mainland. In the future it will be visited more frequently because it now has an airstrip. It is considerably more prosperous than its neighbors, and in most aspects of its culture has caught up with such villages as Unalakleet and Hooper Bay, long under outside influence.

Since, however, the Nunivakers whose reminiscences are recorded here were telling about their childhood, one must remember that the periods covered, even for young people, were before the end of isolation. We cannot assume, though, that the autobiographies are pertinent only to past culture and past events. People who are now trying to live in modern Alaska were shaped in those earlier periods. Although the Festival of Seals' Souls, ordinarily called the Bladder Feast, has not been held for nearly twenty years, individual experiences during those long-past festivals are still influencing behavior. Government employees and other "outsiders" who deal with the people from the Lower Kuskokwim, Nelson Island, and Nunivak Island may find it helpful to know the kinds of experiences that individual Eskimos have had.

Attention should also be given to the texts and pictures in the various publications listed in the Bibliography, most of which deal with the traditional culture. In order to appreciate the experience of individual Nunivakers, one needs to get the look of the place, the feel of the community and of its culture.

Circumstances of Recording. In 1939-40, through almost daily contact I had become well acquainted with most of the individuals whose stories are given here and knew a good deal, by reputation, about all of the people. On my second visit to the island, therefore, it seemed time to try for autobiographies, especially since I had been welcomed back as an old friend. On this visit, the interpreters and I had worked together in giving Rorschach Tests and interviewing. We were ready to work smoothly on this project, and local conditions seemed favorable. Even so, most of those who were asked to tell about their childhood had to think about the request a while before agreeing.

In the summer and fall of 1946, I lived alone in a wanigan, a cabin on a sled, placed between the village and the Reindeer Project buildings. This provided the necessary privacy for the telling of personal stories. The older people could come during the day when children were in school; the youngsters would come after school; and the youths would visit in the evening.

Interpreters were used as indicated for each autobiography; their English names are changed here since they occasionally figure in the stories. The man called Ernest Norton was especially helpful because of his knowledge of genealogies, his interest in language and religious belief. He was not a vigorous hunter but rather a mystic, a disturbed, complex, intelligent person, who perhaps did not have the intensity of expression or was not born into the right family to become a shaman. (He became a lay preacher.) I am no less grateful to him and to all the interpreters than to the biographers. Both types of participant in this project were paid by the hour, though they could not earn as much from me as they earned at the Reindeer Project. Money, therefore, provided one motive for cooperating, and for a few people who could not work much at the project, perhaps a strong one, but for most biographers not the only one. Other motives undoubtedly varied from person to person: anxiety to explain oneself, friendliness toward the writer, obligation to the interpreter who served as go-between. I do not pretend to know the mixture in each case.

In Nunivak culture there is little precedent for an autobiography, especially a long detailed one. Personal stories, like the traditional stories, are succinct narratives. There is little description of scene or of actors' feelings or other elaboration on the outline of events. In the excitement immediately after a fearful event, there will be a full recounting of it. A person who has had a prolonged ordeal, such as being adrift on an ice floe, or who has observed something miraculous will retell the story of it to new people many times. Even so, there is remarkably little embellishment. Formerly, in songs and in presentation of a gift in the ceremonial house, to honor a man's own or his relatives' achievement, there would be some reference to this achievement or other big event in family history. But there were not long boastful accounts in the ceremonies. Since everyone knew the story, it appeared that a reminder was sufficient and most of the story was implied.

Despite the constant flow of gossip, most people have been reluctant to speak out against another to an outsider. Most people also inhibit the emotion of their own tragedies and refrain from inquiring into other people's. Only on intense ceremonial occasions would there be, in the past, a general emotionalism. Today, except in public confession in church, the release of self-restraint does not take the form of prolonged talk. In the Moravian Church on the neighboring mainland, lay preachers and other elders will "bear witness" with long personal accounts, and this is not unknown in the local Swedish Evangelical Church. This, however, is a new development.

Giving a chronological autobiography was, therefore, artificial. In 1946, Nunivakers had not yet taken to reading novels and biographies or even short stories. Although the old story-telling was being weakened, the new forms had not yet been well established.

Nevertheless, despite limitations in the personal histories, there is still a strong argument for this field technique. People revealed in them much that had never been revealed to me in response to questioning. They were especially valuable in communication with the elderly people, since without a really good knowledge of the language the student cannot elicit in conversation a long personal anecdote or statement of feelings. Revelations in casual conversation with the young people were possible, but with the older people a more formal situation including a trusted interpreter had to be arranged.

Partly because of my own interest in childhood and partly because of a sincere desire to reassure these people, I told them that they need not extend their reminiscences beyond childhood. They could keep the whole thing at a safe distance from the present. They were urged to begin with their earliest memories, then carry the story just as far as they wished.

I did not try to create the mood and relationship of the psychoanalyst's office, or, on the other hand, to conduct an interview. So long as the subject was talking freely and his account was reasonably clear, I said nothing. If he came to a full stop or if he wandered off into cultural generalizations, I occasionally inserted a question, as brief and unobtrusive as possible. When one person told, for example, how the shaman called upon his spirits, he was asked, "Could you hear them?" Sometimes it was hard to tell whether the subject was trying to avoid talking about himself or whether he was really talking about himself, by telling those practices and customary ideas that somehow expressed indirectly his own feelings or anxieties. Where I had a strong impression of the latter, a note to this effect is inserted. For the remainder, the reader must decide for himself.

On the 1955-56 visit, conditions also were favorable for getting personal data. I flew to and from the island with young men going home from their jobs in Bethel to spend the Christmas holidays and, while there, was hospitably entertained at the teacherage. The teachers, then in their fourth year of service on the island, knew all its recent news. They and old friends among the Nunivakers were glad to bring all accounts up to date.

Presentation. All autobiographies that were obtained are presented, even though some are fragmentary. Those that are fragmentary supplement the longer ones (e. g., Christine's relatives), provide contrasts, or illustrate special interests and problems of youth. Numerous biographies also were recorded. The most instructive ones are included here.

Notes are keyed to narratives by paragraph numbers. To explain all the items of culture in these personal materials would require repeating much ethnography already available. Hence, only occasionally do the notes explain customs and cultural values. They have been written for four principal purposes (1) to explain specific circumstances, places, people where allusions are unclear; (2) to describe the narrator's reactions and probable feelings, from my observation of him and information from other people; (3) to fill obvious or significant gaps in the narrative; (4) to present, where it seems helpful, my interpretation of behavior described by the narrator, an interpretation based either on long-term experience with the community or upon data pertaining specifically to the biography's subject.

Genealogies are given to show the actual variation in family structure, as well as to help explain references in the autobiographies. Because of the daily habit of teknonymy, free use of numerous nicknames, and reluctance to tell "real names," to mention the deceased, or to talk about marriages that were disapproved, it was difficult to verify the genealogies. They were put together through a total of about fifteen months, with frequent rechecking of informants' statements and of inadvertent revelations in other contexts. Even with their errors and omissions, the genealogies still are more valuable than any other kind of data in demonstrating the complexity of kinship on the island.

The Rorschach Tests were interpreted independently by Dr. Eugenia Hanfmann and Dr. Alice Joseph as part of research in the Department of Social Relations, Harvard University, experimenting with a rating checklist. This was used to see whether the raters could give a more precise statement of the subject's personality, as revealed by the Rorschach protocol, than often is given, to provide an objective measure of their agreement (since the form of interpretation was specific and limited), and to state the basis of each trait rating. Although I knew the two raters' impressions of this Eskimo group as a whole after their work on the Rorschachs, I did not discuss individual subjects with them or look at their ratings or comments on individuals until after all work on these personal histories was done, including the writing of the sequels. To save space, individual ratings on the personality-trait lists are not given in full but are summarized, with comparison of the two raters' statements on these subjects. (For more information on the Rorschach project, the reader may consult Lantis, 1953, pp. 140-45.)

Nunivak folklore is full of stock characters, like "the young man of marriageable age," "the shaman whom people feared," and "the stepmother." All these characters appear in the biographies, but here they are also individuals, with conflicting motives and vacillating action, yet with a form in each life.

Acknowledgment. The fieldwork in 1946 was made possible by a grant from the Arctic Institute of North America. The shorter work in 1955-56 was adjunct to a village sanitation survey for the Public Health Service, Department of Health, Education, and Welfare.

Thanks are given to present or former employees of the Bureau of Indian Affairs, Department of the Interior: Mr. Paul Winsor, Mr. Robert Gibson, Mr. and Mrs. Herman Turner, and Mr. and Mrs. A. L. Judish. Eskimo missionaries of the Swedish Evangelical Church also were hospitable and cooperative. Finally and most importantly, the writer is grateful to a considerate, helpful, and responsible community: Mekoryuk, on Nunivak Island.

NOTES

Material in brackets was inserted by the writer; material in parentheses was given by the narrator as an explanation to writer or interpreter.

Sentences tended to be short and choppy because of problems in interpreting. The translation is assumed to be simpler than the original Eskimo.

Kin terms, words for "shaman," "spirit," and a few other terms hard for the interpreter to translate were usually given in Eskimo but have been translated here by the writer.

All English names have been changed to protect the Nunivakers, especially the young people who have left the island and moved into a larger society. Eskimo personal names and nicknames and the names of villages and camps have been retained so that the serious student can identify these if necessary. Personal names have been partially Anglicized in the text, and their phonetic spellings are given in an appendix. The only sounds that are unusual to English speakers or are difficult to indicate are the following. (The symbol used in the text is in parentheses.) The voiceless l (L); the deep rolled g (G) which Danish linguists recording Eskimo generally write as r but American linguists write as the Greek gamma; the ng (N) sound as in English "singer"—the g is never pronounced separately after η; and an indefinite vowel, as in English "but," here generally written as an unaccented a, occasionally as an unaccented u. Other vowels have values close to those of Spanish.

CONTENTS

Introduction   v

The Oldest Man on the Island

Daniel   3

A Woman of Secure and Prosperous Family

Christine   29
Zachary (Christine's Uncle)   43
Nu'san (Christine's Mother)   49
Paul Scott (Christine's Brother)   52

Three Men Who Were Not Prosperous

Edwin Larson   65
Luther Norton   70
Ralph Johnson   74

Four Young Hunters

Oliver   83
Ethan   91
Dick Lewis   98
Frederick Matthew   104

The Shaman

Richard Chappel   113

The Woman Shaman and Her Family

Helene Stephen   131
Rachel   139
Lydia   143
Nicholas   148

Scandal

Virginia Cannon   153

Ten Years Later   160

Conclusion   167

Appendixes

Appendix A. Rorschach Tests   175
Appendix B. Genealogies   189

Bibliography   215

FIGURES

1. Example of Daniel's carving   4
2. One type of boy's dish   55
3. Mask representing a dog, carved by Luther   72
4. Examples of personal variations in bow and
   stern design in kayaks   85
5. Child's large model kayak   87
6. Ethan's sketches of sea animals   93
7. Drawings made by Richard   115

MAP

Nunivak Island   facing page 3

THE OLDEST MAN ON THE ISLAND

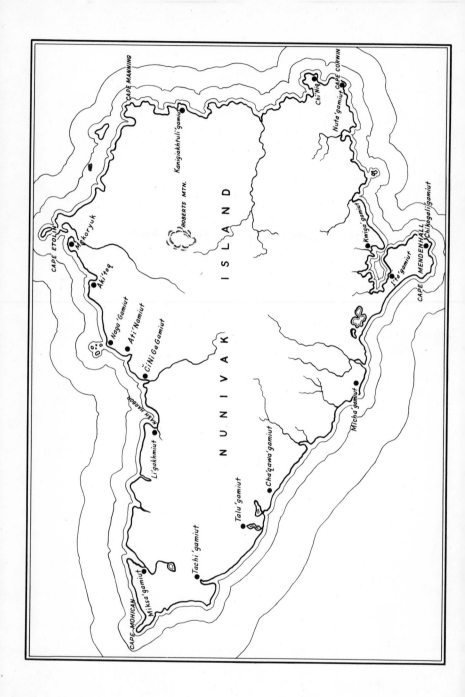

DANIEL

Ernest Norton, Interpreter

Everyone agreed that Daniel was the oldest man on the island. Most people thought he was about eighty-five years old. I surmised, from his own age at marriage and the ages of his children, that he was not over eighty. His memory undoubtedly did go back to the 1870's, possibly to the 1860's. He was, in 1946, somewhat bent and always used a long staff to assist him in walking, yet he appeared and acted remarkably healthy, alert, well controlled, usually with a touch of humor. He worked at the reindeer slaughtering plant, moving slowly and carefully, yet doing adequately his job of pushing entrails out of the chute.

Daniel and the wife of his mature years, who was still living, had had seven children and had done better than most families in keeping their children alive. Aside from his age and the size and vigor of his family, which other Nunivakers remarked, Daniel was notable only for his ivory carving. This had a style perhaps unique among western Eskimos. From walrus teeth, not tusk, he made interesting compositions of separate small bent-kneed human figures, with their animals, houses, boats and other gear. These were not elaborate or elegant, but they showed realistic observation of Nunivak life, and they had a simple charm.

Daniel's account presents Nunivak life before the coming of white men and their epidemics. He apparently had come from a family that was average in many ways. It was neither wealthy nor poor. His close relatives were not shamans, not crippled, or otherwise set apart.

His autobiography is as remarkable for what it omits as for what it includes. At the end are several items that he failed to include on his own initiative, but which I learned by questioning him and others. There are references in other autobiographies to Daniel's wives and children.

3

Figure 1. Example of Daniel's carving from walrus tusk and teeth, done in 1940. His style and composition of work groups and festival groups have been unique among Alaskan carvers. Activities shown, counterclockwise: man cutting up seal on ice; man preparing to cut up walrus, with knife, basket and meat-hook beside him; man chopping drift log with modern axe; man using modern saw; man carrying wood (to kayak builders?); man adzing piece of wood near ceremonial-house entrance; four men working on kayak frame. Height of tallest figure: 1 3/4 inches. (For another example, see Lantis, 1946, p. 190, Fig. 29.)

1. First thing I remember, I was at Nagokigina´gamiut. I was sitting on my mother's lap, sucking at her breast. My mother told me we were going to a sealing camp. She took me out, put me on a sled. Then I forgot.

2. When I remembered next, I was in the entranceway. Some woman I didn't know led me into the kazigi. The men pulled me up [through the floor entrance] and put me on the log [at the edge of the men's sleeping places]. I saw two men lying on the bench. One was Aiya´qsaq. I knew him. I didn't know the other man. Then I forgot.

3. Next time I remembered, I was on sand dunes beside a pond. My father was making the bow of an umiak from driftwood. I asked my father to make me a little kayak. I don't remember whether I got the kayak.

4. We went to Tachi´gamiut. I went in the kazigi and saw my
uncle making a large model of a kayak.

5. I was born at Tachi´gamiut, west of Nash Harbor, and that
was my home all the time I was a boy.

6. My father took me out in a kayak. We went under a cliff; I
looked up and saw caribou for the first time. (This was at Cape
Mohican.) There were two caribou. I wondered if the caribou had
bushes on their heads. That's what I thought.

7. (I started hunting caribou with a bow when I was very young.
I was younger and smaller than any of the boys going out hunting
now. I was so small that I could hardly carry a shoulder of caribou although I used both my hands, but a man could carry a shoulder with one hand.)

8. That time, my father went on to Miksa´gamiut. I saw two of
my uncles there. They had sons and daughters and sons-in-law.
Qo´Goyakh was one of my uncles. He was nicknamed Chaskota´gakh
by his joking-friend. The brother of Qo´Goyakh was Tu´chian. (He
was murdered later.) Their sister was ANa´win, their only sister.
They took me to Nash Harbor in a kayak. They had a seal net and
caught many seals. In the winter I went back to my home on the
south side, to Nagokigina´gamiut. We went on to Chikogali´gamiut
after a few days.

9. In the spring, I had a good time there. I had a pet puppy.
I had a cap made of white fox with the tail on it. I was so small,
the tail dragged on the ground. Many kayaks came on a calm day.
When they arrived, my father told me one of the men was Uya´likh,
father's brother to me. Another uncle, UNu´yaGa´Lagia, from
the mainland, was a trader. These people were not from Nelson
Island, they were from the mainland beyond Nelson Island. They
left one morning. I went up on a hill, and others too, to watch the
people leaving. I saw Uya´likh—he was slow joining the others who
were leaving. I called to him as hard as I could that the others
were leaving him. People laughed at me for this. Uya´likh joined
the others and they all left.

10. When I was a small boy many people came from the mouth
of the Kuskokwim to the villages on the south side. Only men came,
they stayed a while and went back. They came to buy ivory and oil.
They came often, by kayak.

11. Once when people came from the mainland, a Nunivak woman
fell down a cliff on the west side and was killed. The mainland people helped Nunivak people bury her on top of the cliff. Nunivakers
didn't know whether they came as enemies or not. There was no
war in my lifetime, but Nunivakers were very afraid of mainland

people. They were afraid of attack. Some mainland people came
to hunt caribou, but they didn't come often.

12. Then my family went to fish camp. We caught lots of fish
and dried them. Then we went to Cha´qawa´gamiut. We caught
many trout there and stored them. Then we started for Nash Harbor. (Dried trout was piled on the ground, with a rock wall around
it. It was sealed with clay at the corners and covered with rocks.
Stone box for storage: kachi´tat. Fish stored this way: kohlut.)

13. We stayed at Kaya´gayeli´gamiut. We could not go around
Cape Mohican because of a storm. People carried the kayaks on
their backs to Nash Harbor. They carried all the things along.
I walked where the grass was long and got mud in my eyes from
the dust. Many other people were going, too; they were going to
a sealing place out from Nash Harbor. We stopped on the tundra
one night. The next day (we were still on the way to Nash Harbor),
we met two men from Li´gakhmiut (Nash Harbor) wearing puffin
parkas. They were messengers for a ceremony. I thought that
Nash Harbor was a big village, biggest on the island. We stopped
outside the village and people from the village brought out food to
"treat" me. My mother told me we were going to have a ceremony.
That evening they lighted up the big kazigi, called Agomali´nakh
because it was old. (It means "place that is rotten." Refers to the
old wood in the kazigi. But it wasn't rotten or broken down.) [Kazigi
is pronounced approximately ka´zgee.] That kazigi was close to
the river bank; there were many houses beside it. After they lighted
it, they had a dance. It was the first time I had seen this. Everyone had hurried in to Nash Harbor after they met the messengers
inviting them to the feast. They had been slow before this.

14. When winter came, they took me about a mile from Nash
Harbor to a seal-net camp, called Ogaska´gamiut. My father put
out a new seal net. When all the ice came, they took up the nets
and had the Bladder Feast at Nash Harbor.

15. When they took up the seal nets, they had a little dance before
the Bladder Feast, called "Beginning for Drumming," Chaoya´Ni-
chakhlu´tn. Then there was drumming until the end of the Bladder
Feast. Another day, they made new songs in the evening, with the
lights out. Many evenings the men sang new songs. They also made
new dishes. When the dishes were finished, one evening they put out
the lights and called on the shamans to call up creatures from the
sea, and to bring good weather and bring tom-cods and other fish.

16. Next morning, people went out of the kazigi even though it
was very dark and prayed to their i´noGos and Ki´Lkas.

17. They came back in, everybody came in. One man stood up, took a rock into each corner. He motioned as if to touch it to the corner but did not actually touch. The second time, he dropped the stone on the floor in each corner as hard as he could. Then he went to the center and threw the stone down as hard as he could. The man who did this was a specially clean man who had no relative die in the past year. (He couldn't eat, he couldn't sleep with a woman, he had no sins. Chiefly, he couldn't have any connection with a dead person.)

18. The man sat down. People lighted many lamps; they brought in the new dishes, rubbed them with colored shavings, painted them while they sang new songs. Men who had babies born that year made a new dish for the baby. They brought in valuable things, traded them for wood. When the dishes were finished, they dried them with the heat of a sweat bath, then covered them with seal oil to make them smooth. (Dishes are sticky with native paint unless fixed this way.) Old people gave caribou tallow to others to oil the dishes.

19. Next day they started the Bladder Feast. They brought in wild celery, rocks, and dry grass. Then they brought in the [sea mammal] bladders and ice cream. When they inflated the bladders and hung them up, they also hung the first little birds of the boys [i. e. , killed by the boys]. The father of each boy hung up an oogruk skin or something valuable beside the birdskin. At this Bladder Feast at Nash Harbor, my first little bird was hung up.

20. After three days, the men gathered the bladders together in one bunch and put them in the entranceway. Next morning we woke up early. The men told us, little boys and girls, to have a tug o' war. Those who won got a prize. Then they made little drums. When a man finished one, the other men gave him a little prize. In the evening they made the wooden lamp frame, called koga'q-muNoakh, then they sang.

21. After three nights, early in the morning they went out and prayed to their i noGos. We went in again. The men sat on the bench. Every woman brought in a bundle of straw for her husband or son. The women sat on the floor under the bench. From her bundle, a woman would take a few straws, knot them, and give them to her husband and sons.

22. One woman would throw a bundle on the middle of the floor, saying, "This is my husband's bladders' mat if he [i. e. , the seal's spirit] goes with the bladder [back to the sea]. " Her husband also put down a mat for the bladders. The sons did the same for their

little birds or their small seals. They did the same for the men who were dead because they might be cold if they had gone with the bladders under the sea.

23. When there was lots of grass on the floor, they took every child, boy or girl, and hid them under the grass. Some children would cry although people did not try to frighten them. Then they put the children back in their places. They gathered up the grass in one place.

24. Old men, maybe two or five, sat down on the floor, each man with a little drum. The people put a lamp in front of them and a lamp in the entranceway. The old men pointed with their drums, called o-o-o-o-o-Gas, drawn out as long as possible. They called that toward the left front corner—called a;a;wao;a;wao;a;wao toward the entrance.

25. Two men stood up, they took a long stick and swept the grass with one end of the stick, then the other. It was supposed to be a bird sweeping with its wings. They jumped up a little. One man swept, then gave the grass to the other man.

26. Then a man stood up with two young boys (need not be his own). They sat down beside the entrance. When the old men saw these three, one said, "Look at that eider with young ones." The other old man said, "We have no spear to spear those eiders." After the three returned to the bench, the old men lamented that they did not catch the ducks.

27. One man came from the back of the kazigi, bending over, beating a little drum behind his back. One old man would say, "What's that?" The other would sing, "That's ni´naka´makh." (I don't know what that is.) He returned to his seat.

28. Another man stood up with many children; they went beside the entrance. Another man went outside. Those beside the entrance danced like eiders. The other man came in wearing a rain parka. He scared the children, who ran to their fathers. The old men scared them by crying out, "What is that coming in?" They said, "It's a spirit!" When the spirit came in, one man stood up with a child who had a little rod in his hand. The man took the child toward the spirit. The child tried to break the grass hanging down from the forehead of the spirit (he was the spirit of oogruk). As soon as the boy touched the grass, the spirit went out.

29. The spirit came in again, his sleeves tied on his head. He flapped his arms. He was the spirit of Ka´valu´lukh [also a bearded seal]. They gave the children to the spirit; for example, an old man would give his grandson to the spirit. (All year, mothers

threatened naughty children with the coming of this spirit.) The spirit would pretend to take the children out. Their grandfathers and joking-partners would laugh at the children.

30. Only men who were clean were chosen to dance and do these special things.

31. When the spirit went out, two men went out with little wooden buckets. They hollered outside around through the village. They brought in a little salt water, went around sprinkling a little on the floor, all around the kazigi. Children followed the men who were doing that. They poured what was left into the entranceway. When they finished, all men and women stood up and painted their faces with soot, called "sacred smoke." Every family painted the face differently.

32. Two men made a hole in the ice. The poorest man in the village gathered up the grass, put it in the lamp frame, took it out, set fire to it and burnt it all up. People in the kazigi asked if it all burned well. When he answered yes, then all the people went out and went around the fire (all men and women). The ones carrying birds (the boys themselves) threw them in the fire. The bladders were put down under the sea. Sometimes people made three holes in a line out from the shore [i. e., at right angles to the shore]. Clean people threw their bladders in the hole farthest from shore, unclean people nearest shore. If all were clean, they made five holes. A clean person is pi´dhliNokh. After they put the bladders down, they sang.

33. I always was the last to go back in the kazigi because I had such long songs. When I went in, the others already had removed their clothes. All the men took off all their clothes; they went to the entrance and rolled backward across the floor. They put their clothes on the floor and rolled on them. The young men stood up and played tag around the inside of the kazigi, youngest to oldest. When one caught a joking-partner, he slapped him on the back. Then the little children played tag. (They wore clothes.)

34. Women brought dishes of food to their husbands. They ate and slept.

35. That evening, they put up the lamps and had a little dance. Women brought in little dishes. When they were through dancing, the men ate. The dance was the end of the Bladder Feast. They slept.

36. In the morning they had a sweat bath; all the men gave wood. Two wealthy men brought in wood; each made a cane, painted with stripes. They put dog hide around the middle of the cane. They

put them at a back corner, on the wall. One man took one cane, another man took the other cane. This meant they would be messengers.

37. The messengers prepared for the journey. The wealthy men gave them food and other things for the journey.

38. When a messenger was ready, people asked the wealthy man which man he would send for. He answered, he wanted rich men from other villages. He promised the messenger that he would visit the other wealthy man if that man would come to visit him. The messengers went out.

39. We didn't have a Messenger Feast every year. Sometimes in winter, sometimes in summer it was given. A man invited one village at a time. Then that village would invite the first village, in return.

40. When I was a boy, the wealthy man in my village was Aiya'q-saq, father's father of my wife. When I was a young man, the wealthy man was Chiku'Lka'Gakh.

41. Some years ago, Mekoryuk people sent messengers to Nash Harbor and to the south side to invite people. The south side people would send messengers early before the north side people pulled up their nets in the fall. They did not get seals so long on the south side. North side people sent messengers later.

42. When the messenger arrived at the other place, older men in the kazigi asked him what man he was after. The messenger would say, "The wealthy man told me his joking-partner (or serious partner) should go to see him."

43. The village made up new songs after the messenger left their own village. All the people learned the new songs. The messenger would return home, usually at night. (When I was messenger, I would yell and wake everyone up when I returned. The old men in the kazigi would call "ka'vagakh" [messenger] to me two times. They asked, "Will the guest come?" I answered, "He might come without anything," teasing them. I would not return home until just before the guests came.) That evening we would have a good time, have races.

44. One man stood up the next morning; he prepared to receive the guests. Usually he put on women's clothes, just to make people laugh or because women's clothes are fancier. When that man went out, the young men followed him out to have a race with the visitors. They also got ready to race. When they met, they raced, sometimes as much as six miles.

45. Two men would go ahead to meet the sleds of the visitors while other runners waited, but just when they reached the visi-

tors, they turned back and the race started. Sometimes the visitors won the race. When Nash Harbor people came to Mekoryuk, runners would go out about three miles to meet them.

46. Once, when I was a boy on the south side of Nunivak, I saw runners coming, two good runners among the visitors. Our village had one good runner. The two good runners in the morning ate a lot of good seal oil and other food. Our man did not eat or drink. The two visitors beat everyone: they ran the whole length of the lake, about ten miles. Kiawi´Gakh was the man who ate nothing. Pu´psu´kh and Mani´Ganakh were the other two men. (Pu´psu´kh was father's brother to Arthur's father.)

47. Shamans came out wearing very large masks, to meet the visitors. Shamans among the visitors also wore masks of animals or spirits. When the shamans returned, they took food out and treated the people. After they ate outdoors, we took the guests into the kazigi. They wouldn't let people of our village go in while the visitors were getting ready in the kazigi. They brought in a large log, tied it to the skylight by ropes at the ends. They had a contest in log-jumping by the good jumpers of our village and the guests.

48. The men called the two messengers, told them to gather the visitors in the entranceway. Five of the visitors were brought into the kazigi. (Log-jumping is pagu´kaGakh.) The man swinging the log wore a headdress like a woman's reindeer-hair headdress. People stamped on the ground and yelled as the log swung. Sometimes when a particular visitor would climb on the bench to jump over the log, the log-swinger would not swing the log to him because he was afraid the visitor would hurt him as he swung on the log.

49. When everyone came in, they put a lamp on the stand in each corner, fancy painted stands. They took the drums and sang shamans' songs. Everyone sang, including women and children. (Singing shamans' songs: nula´luni.) They brought a lot of food into the kazigi after singing. Every family brought in its best food.

50. Next morning the visitors went out and got things they had brought for the ceremony. That evening everybody got ready for the ceremony. Guests danced first, starting with the old men and then down to the young men. Each young man would bring in a knife or any little thing that he had made as well as he could, while rich older men brought hides and many good things—big things. Rich men sometimes brought in clothes already made [besides or instead of the skins usually given]. Sometimes the visitors brought in things just for prizes. Before we had white men's things, it

was much harder to get goods for a feast. Everything had to be made by the people themselves. Later, they could buy things to give away.

51. This is the way they did it: a wife and sons and daughters danced while her husband threw down goods. Each visitor brought in little things. Then our village did the same. After they finished dancing, first the guests, then our people spread out the things they had brought in. Usually the local people gave more. If it was good weather, a man of our village would put something on a pole, a visitor would take it down, put up something as good or better. They did that outdoors.

52. Next day, in the daytime, the visitors came out from the kazigi again. The two messengers went with them, took little things from them and put them in the kazigi. The guests came in the kazigi then and everyone came in.

53. People danced with small masks, ordinary masks, not shamans' masks, but men danced according to the way shamans had told them. Messengers then showed the people the things given them by the guests—several things given by the guests. These were divided among our people.

54. We put the visitors on the bench and fed them. When they finished, some of them danced while all the other visitors sang. We did nothing, we just enjoyed the singing and dancing. When they finished, all of us left the kazigi and the visitors prepared for the ceremony, with drums and masks. They used ours—they didn't bring their own masks. The two messengers stayed with them to help them. Each family in our village came in to dance; they danced family by family. Then people put out the lights in the corners; they lighted the lamp in the center and ate. Then we slept.

55. Next day we had a good time singing shamans' songs and dancing with masks. When we finished, we put the masks up in a row above the entrance to let the guests see them. One shaman tried to get animals from the sea. People hung a mask of the animal on the back wall of the kazigi. We hung the big masks that the shamans wore when they went out to meet people, sideways in the center of the kazigi.

56. Then we had a sweat bath, all men of the visitors and our village. We practiced the new songs that we had heard the visitors sing. That was the end.

57. When spring came, we moved to Tachi´gamiut. In the summer when we children were playing outside the village, I heard that two boats were coming. They were Ulu´pi and Ili´esi, the first

wooden boats I had seen. They were schooners, with only sails, no engine. The first gun on Nunivak was obtained from the men on the boat. Chani´aGa´Lagia(nicknamed Kukhsa´Gan, means "leaking") was the man who got the gun. My father bought a red suit for me—it cost a lot. My brother had lots of red fox that he got in the fall with a big metal bear trap that he had bought at Tununak. He also had bought a metal kettle. My father had paid a new kayak for the trap and kettle. My brother gave his red foxes to father and my father traded them for the red suit.

58. My father brought crackers from the boat. There was some kind of paint on the crackers. I and my brother ate this off the top of the crackers. We put the crackers on a shelf—they got moldy, then we threw them away. We didn't know they were food, that we could eat them. Men brought tobacco from the boats. They had had tobacco before; they got it at Nelson Island. Russians had brought it there before I was born.

59. Before this, when I was a little boy, no white man had come to Nunivak yet. Nunivak people never had even seen wooden boats. Once when I was out hunting caribou with some men, we saw two ships off the west end of the island, the first we ever saw. They did not come in to Nunivak.

60. Men from the ship that came in to Tachi´gamiut built a boat while they were there. I think that was the first ship to come to shore. Then after that, there were many ships hunting whales.

61. One time, not far west of Mekoryuk, out here on the north side of the island, a ship was grounded and wrecked. It happened when there still was ice all along shore. Before the ice was all gone [i. e., before very long], another ship came and took the men away. Nunivakers got things from the wreck for a long time.

62. After the two ships left, my family went to Cha´qawa´gamiut. In the fall we moved to Micha´gamiut.

63. I was the youngest. It was a big family. I had one brother and many sisters, all older than I. At that time, I was growing up. I was going to have my first kayak that winter. We had the Bladder Feast there, three families: Pukhta´oGokh's family, my family, and Tutu´men, my father's brother. When the Bladder Feast ended, my father finished the kayak frame. He was helped by Ki´Giwan, my father's nephew. I was about the size of Rickie [about eleven years old]. When they painted the kayak frame, they made me fast one day—eat nothing.

64. In spring we moved to Kani´khligamiut [where?]. We did not get many seals. Pukhta´oGokh got only one. Late in the spring, my family moved to Chikogali´gamiut, hunting walrus and mukluk.

Before we moved from spring camp, my uncle killed one caribou. After he got the caribou, he piled the meat and left some of it because he had no sled. White fox came around. My uncle hid behind a block of snow; when the foxes came to eat the meat, he shot them. I stayed alone with my mother when the men went to Chikogali´-gamiut. I took my new kayak out on the ground when the snow was melting and practiced paddling it on the ground.

65. Before my father returned, a south wind blew hard. It blew ice on shore. I went along the shore and a little way from the village I saw a baby spotted seal. I tried to beat it to death but I couldn't. My mother came, helped me hit it and killed it. I went on and saw another. Together, we killed it. I went on, I saw a young ring seal and we killed it, too. Those were the first seals I ever got—three in one day. My mother removed the bladders when we brought them into the village. I put them on the shelf in the little side room of the house. I didn't blow them up because I didn't know how. When my father returned, he inflated them and he made new songs for them. I fasted until the next day—that day I got the seals. I didn't have to remove my clothes or change my clothes.

66. Sometimes a boy, when he got his first seal, wore old woman's clothes and slept in them the first night after getting a seal. He took them off the next day. A woman took off her ornaments if her first son got his first seal. My mother did not do this because she had many children before me.

67. In the summer we moved to fish camp. I always followed my father when he went fishing. Some other boys would not walk in water, fishing, after they got a seal.

68. My father made a small net for puffins. When autumn came, we moved to Cha´qawa´gamiut with nets and walrus-hide ropes [to catch the puffins on the cliff rookeries]. I think summer and fall were long when I was a boy. Now they are short. Many people came there. Then we moved to Kaya´gayeli´gamiut. I did not take my kayak: we put it in a sheltered place. Then we moved on to Nash Harbor. There we made floats for the seal nets and spread the nets. We had two long nets and got many seals.

69. After we pulled up the nets, we had the Bladder Feast at Nash Harbor. When it was finished, we stayed at Nash Harbor a while. When my father brought dried fish from Cha´qawa´gamiut, he also brought my kayak. Many people went out to the sealing camps [in the spring], but my family and Tachi´Lka did not move.

70. I went out alone with my father to hunt seals. We went toward Cape Mohican. It was very foggy, so we did not go out to the

ice. We saw one spotted seal, my father shot at it, missed it. The seal appeared again, my father reloaded his gun and shot it. He planned that if he did not hit the seal with the gun, he would get it with the big harpoon. This was the first time I went out to the ice to hunt. We went further and met two men. At evening, the four of us returned to land. When we got back to land, my father gave half of the spotted seal to others in honor of the first hunting by his son although I did not kill the seal. (A man would give away a seal if he got it when his son was hunting with him, as if the son got the seal himself.) It was stormy when we approached the village. My father held up his paddle to show the village that he caught something.

71. When we went into the kazigi, my mother brought in the bladder of the spotted seal and half the skin.

72. My father went down on the south side. I wanted to go along very much but my father wouldn't take me. Before my father returned, my mother and the remainder of the family moved to Miksagamiut. Next summer, my father came there also. My father had caught only one mukluk but he had got many other seals. My father got sick that summer and died after a few days. My family stayed at this village a long time.

73. That fall my cousin came and got me and took me to the south side. None of my sisters had married yet. We slept on the tundra while walking down to the south side. My cousin made a bed of dry grass for me. In the morning it was snowing. We came to Micha´gamiut. We were going to move to another village but it was snowing. We prepared to go when it got calm. One dog had pups and I liked one of them, with a white collar, and I put it inside my parka. My aunt told me not to take the puppy but I kept it anyway. When we arrived on the other side of the lagoon, we slept on the bank of the lagoon. One of my uncles had a new wife but they still were living with his mother. Next day my two uncles got their kayaks. We had a bad storm, so we couldn't leave the lagoon. The puppy had no mother to suckle, and I fed it human food. We moved on to Nagokigina´gamiut when the storm passed and slept in my father's house there.

74. I was unhappy when I had to go down on the south side with my relatives. I didn't want to leave my mother.

75. I had an aunt there, father's sister. We got lots of flounders. We filled big wooden dishes many times. Sometimes they speared loons too, when they went fishing for flounders. My uncle gave a loon to his wife. After she removed the skin of the loon, she made ice cream for the people, in honor of the loon.

76. In the spring we moved to Chikogali´gamiut. Pukhta´oGokh made me a new kayak. That spring my grandfather went with me to hunt seals by kayak. He was named A´ganaGai´yakh. (My uncle, father's brother, was named Lukhtusi´Gakh.) One day my grandfather went out with me. We saw two kayaks, one of them loaded with seals. When the kayaks met, another man, named A´ganaGai´-yakh too, had one seal. He said he had seen two seals but had missed one. That evening we went home.

77. When the ice melted, people went out and drove beluga into the bay: they got lots of beluga. They speared them from kayaks. (Another time Russell's father speared a beluga when he was out hunting with me. The float was going so fast after the beluga was harpooned and was trying to get away that my kayak nearly was upset by the float. Russell's father picked me up and put me in his kayak so I wouldn't upset.) That other time, the men told me to spear a beluga but I wasn't fast enough to hit one. Then we took the meat and blubber ashore.

78. The people sent two messengers to Nelson Island, one named Taku´kasakh, Ernest's great-grandfather, and one named Na´n-nokhka´Lagia. This was at the beginning of summer. People made up new songs after the messengers left. After many days the two messengers returned. Next day they went out to race with the visitors with kayak. While we were waiting in ChiNi´gakhLugakh, the visitors came. Two men went out in kayaks to meet them, others waited on shore ready to run away if necessary. I was one of the two who went out in kayaks. We used big paddles.

79. The four of us young men who were going to race stayed apart in one place but the other people went to meet the guests when they came ashore. When we raced, I was way behind the others. A kayak with a Nelson Islander passed me although I paddled as hard as I could. Then another Nelson Island man, with a white kayak, came up. But the other Nunivaker won. He was my father-in-law later (my present wife's father).

80. One Nelson Island man put a young man's paddle up on a pole crosswise and put an oogruk (mukluk) skin on it. They had many baby mukluk skins on the pole at this ceremony. Naka´Gakh put his son's paddle on a pole and put the largest oogruk skin on it. That evening we had the dances. Next morning they made canes for a race. One man brought in a pair of canes. We went out on the tundra to a place named Amiak, about five miles from Chi´Niq. A Nelson Islander won. (We held a stick in each hand when racing.) I ran too; I didn't get very tired and was nearly first.

81. At the end of the Messenger Feast, when there was calm

weather, the visitors went home. Then my family went to fish camp. My mother came while we were there. I went with her when she returned to Miksaʹgamiut and lived there a long time.

82. When I was a young man, we usually moved to Tachiʹgamiut in the spring. My mother had no husband. At Tachiʹgamiut I got my first oogruk. My uncles told me to get every kind of animal in the sea before I got married. I was nearly old enough to be married then. When I had caught one of each animal and especially the oogruk, my uncles told me to marry someone, but I didn't want to. They didn't pick out a wife; they just told me to marry.

83. Two men were going to the south side and they took me along with them. We speared ducks and I always hit the ducks first. After a few days on the south side, I came back again. I stopped at a camp because it was storming and stayed three days. On a calm day I went around the coast to Tachiʹgamiut. I told the people at Tachiʹgamiut that there was ice out in the sea. Many men went out to the ice and that evening they returned with spotted seals. The next day I went, too, but I got only one baby spotted seal although others got many. Some of the men then went out fishing for cod and got lots. That was the first fresh fish of the season.

84. Another day when the men went out to the ice, I went with them. I and another man found spotted seals all gathered in one place. The other man had a harpoon, I had only a gun. The man hit one seal with his harpoon. I shot but missed. The other man's line broke and the seal got away.

85. Some men came from the south side to the cliffs to hunt puffins and murres. They told others that I was asked to go down to the south side. I asked my mother and she said yes. I walked, stopping at Chaʹqawaʹgamiut, then went on to Michaʹgamiut. My uncles told me I was to be married. I had no sweetheart and I didn't like the girl my uncles chose for me, but I obeyed and married Ichaʹganin. I took her to Tachiʹgamiut. I wouldn't sleep with her on the way. At Tachiʹgamiut, she brought [Daniel] a dish of good food into the kazigi in another man's dish very early in the morning. I had given her a parka and boots before that. Then we lay together. A man married my sister at the same time.

86. When winter came, my brother-in-law came to get his wife, my sister. He told me I should go with my sister back to my mother's home. I was afraid of my wife's mother, who was a shaman. I was afraid she would keep me from getting animals, by her spirits. So I left my wife even though I liked her now. That spring I hunted without a wife. (My wife was young at that time.)

87. Another man asked me to marry his daughter. I didn't want

her, but my mother told me to marry her, so I did. That wife was so young—I didn't desire her. After one month, I left her. Once I tried to go in to her, but she was scared and cried; so I never slept with her.

88. My mother died and I lived with my sister. Then I got another wife and again she was chosen by another man. I was married to her a long time. I stayed with her because she was a good woman, but I went after other girls. I loved any girl there was around. Then my wife was pregnant. I knew the baby was a female and I left her because I didn't want a girl child. But I can't remember her name. What was her name? I should remember.

89. So then I married Russell's sister-in-law, Joel's mother. I loved her but she left me because some other men told her father that I hated her, so her father took her away. Again, I stayed with my sister.

90. Then I took Jimmie Dennis's father's mother. I loved her and lived with her a long time even though she had no children. I liked her because she got along well with my sister. We lived with my sister a long time.

91. That other wife's name was A´naGaN—I just remembered.

92. When I was a middle-aged man, A´chago´nakh took my sister for his wife. My sister had a daughter. A´chago´nakh married his wife's daughter, that is, my sister's daughter, at the time he married my sister. My wife's mother scolded me because of my sister. I loved my sister, so I left my wife. I took only a box of tools; I left everything else when I left my wife. If my mother-in-law had not scolded me—said bad things against my sister—I wouldn't have left. I had been out hunting; when I came in, my mother-in-law talked mean to me. I left right away.

93. Next time, I married my present wife. I did not expect to be married long. But I kept thinking a long time about leaving her and before I left her, she became pregnant, and I stayed with her. We were living here when my children were born. We lived for a while, though, at Ka´nigiakhtuli´gamiut, after they were born.

94. After I married my present wife, I went to St. Michael once, in a skin-boat, to get white man's goods. Zachary's father had the first plank boat on the island. Edwin Larson's father had a plank boat and sold it to Elizabeth's father. When I was young, almost all men had big skin-boats. Only a few men owned no skin-boat.

95. When I was a young man, I always was sick. After my mother died, I never was sick any more. The only time I was seriously hurt was when I was out in a kayak; I came along shore and went up on shore to look around. I saw a seal. I ran down, fell and broke

my middle finger. My wife's brother was with me—he paddled and took me home. It would have been fixed by a doctor [i. e. , it would have been all right if he could have got to a doctor]. My hand was bad, so I bored into the back of my hand with a metal point, but it still was bad. Then I bored into my wrist and it healed. I also broke my shotgun when I fell.

96. I´mmin, a good hunter, who was nicknamed Chiuta´LiNokh (no ears), pierced my ears. Tachi´Lka pierced my lip. He was my father's joking-partner and my mother's serious partner. My lip was pierced before I got married the first time. Probably I was twenty years old. Young men marry younger now. And children are different now. They're disobedient. When I was a boy, I did what I was told to do, and even when I was a young man.

97. One time Joshua and I took some wood from a pile of wood belonging to Kapu´Gan, Richard Chappel's father, a strong shaman. Kapu´Gan had said he would bring sickness to anyone who took his wood. I got a sore place on my right palm—you can still see it. My whole hand hurt. Joshua also got a sore. Joshua went after Kapu´Gan, accused him of causing the sore. So Kapu´Gan treated him and made him well. But my hand has been bad ever since.

98. Men on those first two schooners took Nunivak women but did not stay long. Many years later, when I was a young man hunting mukluk, a ship was wrecked on the west side. Most of the men went away soon, but two men stayed.

99. Ernest: About those two men—there were two white men and an Eskimo from up north. They had a store at Tachi´gamiut. That man took the wife of a Nunivak man. The Nunivak man came after him with a gun; he shot at him but missed. Then that white man and the Eskimo shot him [the Nunivaker?]. He fell but he continued to live. They shot at him again and again—he was still breathing. Finally they killed him.

100. They took three Nunivak women altogether, and they killed one of them. One of the three women was Edwin Larson's wife's mother [not killed]. The Nunivak woman went on living with the white man even after he killed her husband.

101. That white man killed another Nunivak man. A white fox was stolen from him. He said he would kill the one who stole it. Pa´ogoyukh, Daniel's [only] brother, was the one who stole the fox. People warned him not to go near the store. He sent the fox into the store, offered it in trade. The white men recognized it because the nose-skin was broken. The trader took it and put up an order of goods for Pa´ogoyukh, but he said he would kill him if he ever saw him. Just then, Pa´ogoyukh walked in. That white

man reached for his gun on the back wall. Pa´ogoyukh ran out,
away from the village toward a lake. He was a fast runner. The
white man went up on top of the house, shot and missed. It took
a long time to reload in those days. Pa´ogoyukh was a long way
off when he shot again, but that white man hit him and killed him.
Two of Pa´ogoyukh's father's brothers were in the store when this
happened. One wanted to kill the white man right then. The other
said, wait, kill him later. But they never did kill him.

102. That man came back to Nunivak in 1928. He said he was
a Christian now, he didn't do bad things anymore. Nunivak people
did not know his name.

103. Daniel: Yes, that Pa´ogoyukh was my brother. My son Pa´-
ogoyukh was named for my brother. I wanted to kill the white man
but my uncle wouldn't let me.

104. Ernest: One white man, later, married a woman on the
south side. He liked Nunivak people, he was good to his wife and
kind to all the people. When he went back to the mainland, he said
he would return. For a long time he sent his wife things she would
need. Then he didn't send any more and people heard nothing more
about him. They thought he died—they never knew. He stayed a
year or maybe more.

105. Chu´qa and Russell's wife (his wife now) adopted two of
Daniel's children and both died. Daniel and his wife did well: they
raised all the children they kept. Pa´ogoyukh was married before
he died [i. e., the son reached an age old enough to marry].

NOTES

1. These phrases "I forgot" and "I remembered" are the Nunivak way of saying "I don't remember" and "I remember." Possibly he remembers this particular incident because his mother denied him the breast. He did not describe it as an unpleasant occurrence, however. Since children were nursed a long time, he may have been four years old or older.

2. This may have been the Aiya´qsaq who was the wealthy man of his village in Daniel's early childhood. Nunivakers of past generations seem to have been much impressed by the "wealthy men," the great men, of their childhood.

3. This definitely was a frustration or threat of a frustration. Probably, he either did not get the toy kayak at all or else after delay.

5. This does not mean that the family stayed at Tachi´gamiut even for part of every year. It means evidently that Daniel thought of this village as his home even though he lived at several other villages in his early years.

7. Very few such interruptions in his chronological narrative occurred. He told his story with remarkable concentration and lack of digression. It required more than one session to tell it, yet he went on without apparent break in his thought.

9. Throughout, he stressed his small size. Although short, even for a Nunivaker, his stature was not the explanation for this emphasis. He was the baby of his family and seems to have fancied himself in that role. He was slow in growing up socially, as will be seen.

It is unlikely that his father told him his uncle's "real name" at that time. This probably is a normal memory confusion. If his father did tell him the real name, that was flattering to a child.

Most of the well-adjusted Nunivakers volunteered stories of their embarrassment. In some cases, there were elements of self-punishment or self-pity. The latter was more common because of the child's resentment against adults for misunderstanding him.

10. This information was given in answer to my previous questions regarding people from the mainland.

11. The implication is that the people might have come as enemies, but when there was a death, then they refrained from attack.

In Daniel's childhood there were wild caribou on the island, before the introduction of domestic reindeer.

13. He undoubtedly had been carried into the kazigi from earliest infancy. This was the first dance he recalled, though.

14. A new seal net represented a big investment in time and effort.

15. Ernest: When I was a boy, I used to get sleepy when the lights were out and the men were thinking of their songs. It was very dark.

Like others, Daniel gave the positive, hopeful aspects of ceremonial. In fact most ceremonies seem to have been given in an atmosphere of festivity, success or reassurance of success.

17. This action with the stone nailed the earth down, kept it in place. This also was a positive ritual act, to keep things right with Nunivak.

18. This means making a new design to be painted on the dish or using, for the baby, a design used by an honored grandfather or other elder. These were important happy events in family life. The men who "bought" firewood with valuable gifts were thus the hosts at a sweat bath honoring their infants.

28. Daniel explained that the three spirits represented three bearded seals, a young one, an adult male, and an adult female, appearing in that order. Adults told the children that the spirits were real and dangerous; at the same time told them that they must not be afraid of the spirits. In other words, this was a test.

30. Daniel stressed ritual cleanliness more than anyone else describing the Bladder Feast. This either represents the ancient viewpoint, that younger people have lost, or else it shows a special personal—probably symbolic—significance for him. Perhaps he was chosen at some time as the poorest and "cleanest" man in the village.

32. After this description of sending the seals back under the sea, I asked who the "poorest man" was and whether he was ashamed of being chosen for this office. Daniel said he was a man who caught no seals that year but was ritually clean. He need not be ashamed of being chosen "poorest man." Sometimes the poor man of the village was someone the wealthy man hated and would not help. But also sometimes the poor man got to be a rich man. HlikhchuNu´niakh is the word for "poor man" in this connection. With the great competition in hunting, one can surmise that the man so designated did indeed feel ashamed, unless he was one who could not be expected to go hunting without assistance: perhaps an old man without children or a young man who was an orphan. Despite my curiosity and suspicion, I did not ask Daniel whether he ever had been chosen as "poor man." I was not sure whether he added the statement that the poor man might get rich or whether Ernest added this on his own. In any case, I had a defi-

nite impression that Daniel identified himself with the man in this position.

33. The implicit statement of the wealthy man's control of the village is especially interesting.

35. This probably was the Men and Women's Exchange Feast.

39. This statement of inviting only one village at a time seems to be contradicted elsewhere. Possibly, if the Messenger Feast was given by two men, as in this case, each one invited a village.

42. More than anything else, the Messenger Feast set wealthy men apart from the remainder of the community.

44. Ernest: One time they ran so far that several got tired and fell exhausted. All the fast runners got tired. A slow runner finally passed them and reached the village first.

45. This whole section subconsciously presents the competition in Nunivak life. This competition became a highly personal rivalry in many cases. Although men were engaged in a more active and dramatic competition and often recounted competitive events, women in a more general way also expressed competitiveness.

46. When such a term as "father's brother" was used, it did not necessarily denote father's sibling. The parent's parallel cousins would be treated the same as his siblings.

47. He here resumes the narrative after a digression to tell about a race on another occasion.

51. For the next few paragraphs the account is confused. It can be summarized as follows: both sides danced without masks when they gave presents; then both sides danced, wearing masks, as entertainment.

57. The family moved back to Tachi'gamiut from Nash Harbor. For the next few years Tachi'gamiut and other villages on the west side of the island had more contact with "outsiders" because of the whaling fleet passing by that side of Nunivak. From 1920 onward, villages on the north side had closer contact with the "outside." This scene of the 1870's when Daniel got his red suit was undoubtedly typical of such scenes of first encounter, even though this was not, as Daniel thought, the first ship to come to Nunivak. Daniel's position in the family is indicated by his father's and brother's act in buying him the red suit.

63. This information was his answer to my question. Through most of the autobiography, Daniel stressed his small size and his submission to adults. He probably had an unusually protected childhood, which he sought to prolong. With a strong mother (shown later), older brother, and several older sisters, his attitude is to be expected.

He may have been older. His short stature would explain his visualizing himself as a ten- or eleven-year-old boy.

64. On Nunivak, "mukluk" was used for adult bearded seal instead of the northern term "oogruk." "Levtak" referred to year-old bearded seal.

65. There was no suggestion of hesitation or repugnance in killing the baby seals. Nunivak children are conditioned to an aggressive predatory life from the time they can toddle. They desire intensely to kill animals, and they practice by using slingshot, bolas, and darts against birds, foxes, puppies, anything moving. But again Daniel mentions his juvenilism: he does not know how to blow up the bladders.

68. The importance to the Nunivak boy of his kayak and its gear is shown clearly.

70. The shift from habitual hunting with harpoon to hunting with gun is shown.

There was a magical concept here: if the boy's first seal was given away, he would always catch seals in adulthood.

73. Daniel did not say voluntarily that he was unhappy when he was taken away from his parental family, but his defiant cherishing of the puppy showed his need for love. Hence I asked how he felt when he went to live with his uncles—whether he liked them and enjoyed being with them or whether he disliked living with them— trying to phrase the question so that either a positive or negative answer would sound acceptable. His answer was vigorously and honestly negative, verified by his later behavior.

75. The loon probably was the family totem.

76. These uncles are not the ones mentioned at the beginning of his autobiography. This is his father's family, living on the south side of Nunivak. The other uncles apparently belonged to his mother's family, living on the west side.

81. It is likely that Daniel made his loneliness and unhappiness evident and so convinced his mother that he should return with her. Also, by this time he was old enough to help support her and his sisters. Nunivak children today when unhappy are not outspoken regarding their difficulties, but often they mope. By looking resentful, disinterested in the activities of others, and pouting, they make their attitudes evident. Daniel may have behaved similarly, or he may have made more vigorous appeals to his mother.

82. Daniel's whole affectional life was absorbed by his mother and sisters. One can see the uncles' efforts to make him assume the full masculine role.

83. This probably was a wife-hunting trip, an unsuccessful one.

85. His statement that he had no sweetheart implies that young men usually did have sweethearts before marriage. Although girls supposedly were protected, youths generally found lovers among young women who had been widowed or deserted.

86. Daniel's wife, Icha´ganin, later became a famous shaman herself. The fact that Daniel did not like her would appear at first to be more important than any characteristic of her mother's. Yet Daniel left another wife later because of mother-in-law trouble. He acted rather apologetic for leaving this first wife, especially for the somewhat cowardly reason first given. He justified his action by adding that his wife was young, too young.

88. His sudden excess of virile masculine behavior probably was a reaction to his mother's death as much as to his marriage to a mature woman and expansion of sexual experience.

Overtly, Daniel expressed no guilt for abandoning a good wife when she was pregnant, but perhaps his forgetting her name is an indication that he needed to repress certain feelings and memories. When I looked surprised at his statement of recognizing the foetus's sex, Ernest said matter-of-factly that Eskimos always know such things.

92. One of his sisters partially took his mother's place in his life. Just as he had been submissive to the wishes of his mother and uncles previously, so now his sister came first in all his considerations.

93. Daniel did not mention that any of these women had children by previous marriages. It must have been hard for him to assume the care of children and show strong affection for children until nearly middle age. For example, he did not mention that his present wife brought with her a young daughter by a previous marriage.

94. From here on, all information was given in answer to my questions. To ascertain outside contacts and influences, I asked whether he had gone to the mainland. He had had little experience off Nunivak Island and apparently it had not impressed him or had any basic effect on him.

95. I congratulated him on his evident good health and good fortune in avoiding accidents, and received this very revealing statement regarding his early ill health. Whether his mother kept him in poor health in order to bind him to her, or whether he remained sickly in an effort to hold her solicitude, the statement still is interesting.

97. It was characteristic of Nunivakers, especially the older ones, not to volunteer statements of accidents and epidemics involving themselves. Daniel had not mentioned his poor health in

childhood, although he had implied it by references to getting tired, not winning races, etc. , or the accident to his hand or the bewitching of his hand. One finger was crooked, and he still had a dark spot on his hand.

98. I asked whether the white men took Nunivak women. In his reply, Daniel was thinking of, but did not tell me of, events that still determine social relationships among Nunivakers and between them and the whites. Ernest then told the story of the two white men. As he told it, the men did not stay when the ship was wrecked, but they returned later to stay as traders. The events described probably occurred in the 1890's. Ernest of course was not living then but had heard the story many times. One white man obviously was leader and villain. He was referred to as "that man" or "that white man. " From the appearance of his offspring, one can surmise that he had some Negro blood. Evidently it was Edwin Larson's wife's mother who continued to live with the white man even after the latter had killed her husband, explaining the prejudice against the daughter that I had noted. The mother became a shaman.

101. When Ernest mentioned Pa´ogoyukh and asked Daniel whether this man was his brother, Daniel said yes, then his eyes filled with tears, and he sobbed once. He removed his glasses, wiped his eyes, and gradually recovered. Then Daniel left. Ernest said he was sorry for having made the old man cry. He thought Daniel was crying for his son who had died only a couple of years previously, rather than for the brother who had died long ago.

104. As if to apologize to both Daniel and me and set everything straight, Ernest told of the white man who was sympathetic and generous to Nunivak people, not like "that white man. "

A WOMAN OF SECURE AND PROSPEROUS FAMILY

CHRISTINE GREGORY

Ernest Norton, Interpreter

Christine's family is closer to what most people would consider a normal American family of the middle class than any other on the island in the present generation. She and her brother Paul lived with their own parents until adulthood. They had no step-siblings or adopted siblings. Their parents were happily married, with satisfactory status and economic security. Christine was not married until late in adolescence, unlike most Nunivak girls, who marry at about puberty. Of the seven children she had borne in about seventeen years (her exact age at marriage is not certain), two had died. She had neither given nor taken children in adoption. She and her husband seemed happy together. She showed independence of action, even to the point possibly of dominating her husband. At any rate, she was more anxious to learn English and take a leading part in the church and school and more successful in such things than her husband. He seemed deliberately conservative, clinging to old ways and showing only moderate interest in the new religion. Both were willing to act independently of the community, going to the south side of the island to live by themselves in an abandoned village because the hunting was better there. Both were very ambitious to improve their economic position.

During childhood and youth, Gregory was poor. His father had been crippled; he was described as having had one bad leg and unable to hunt much. Gregory's father had been poor all his life and his paternal grandfather also had been poor. But Gregory's mother's father was a wealthy man and a chief. Gregory had set out to compete with the good hunters. He had a strong drive to become well-to-do and was gradually succeeding.

Their two oldest boys were above average intelligence. Gilbert was unusually alert and active, with quicker response and greater restlessness than most Nunivak children showed. These traits

just at this time were partly attributable to Gilbert's stage of de-
velopment: he was beginning the social and physical transition of
puberty. The next child, Danny, was being negativistic and anti-
social, evidently feeling rejected after having been babied exces-
sively in early childhood. The two youngest children were rather
infantile and dependent, but probably no more than most Nunivak
children of their ages. The eldest daughter, Dorothy, had mar-
ried young because she had become pregnant. She married the son
of the village leader, an immigrant from the mainland. There is
a hint that Christine favored her sons above her daughters.

It was noticeable that Gregory exacted obedience from his boys,
no matter how they might behave toward others. There was some
evidence that the boys feared him, but there was not enough oppor-
tunity to observe them together to be sure of this.

When Christine gave this account, she was about thirty-six years
old, looked younger than her age, with a hearty pink-cheeked ap-
pearance and considerable charm.

1. The first thing I can remember was when I was maybe three
years old or even less, before Paul was born. We lived at Cape
Mendenhall, not I´ta´gamiut, but Chikogali´gamiut. We came to
Mekoryuk to attend the Bladder Feast. That was the first time
I had traveled by dog team so far as I remember. We did not follow
the coast, we came right across the island. When we got to Mekoryuk or just before we reached here, the young men had a race. I
don't remember anything of the feast itself.

2. On the way home, people slept in the snow: they packed snow
in a big cloth [probably heavy canvas], then slept inside the cloth,
as in a sleeping bag. We kept warm. Other people were traveling
with us. Pearl's mother? Harmon? I don't remember. At that
time, very few lived at Mekoryuk and Nash Harbor. Everyone
lived on the south side, so the people returned there. We had something to eat made of flour. I liked it and I wanted more, but my
parents wouldn't give it to me. I cried hard, and I got more.

3. At about that same time, my family went to Paimiut. I saw
a man there with a red cloth shirt with white fox tails sewed on it.
I never had seen such a thing before. I can't remember any more
from that time.

4. When I was about the age of Mildred [i. e., five or six years
old], I remember I was playing with Adam, Gregory [now her hus-
band], and Judith, Chris's sister. Two kayaks were approaching.

I got in a fight with Gregory and made his nose bleed [much laughter]. In the kayaks were my father and Lewis—at that time he was a young fellow. They brought in several seals; they had been up at Cape Manning hunting.

5. Then I don't remember any more until at the Bladder Feast one time. Just before the men painted new dishes and composed new songs, people all went into the kazigi—everybody. They put on gut parkas and went outside. The old men drummed and sang. They said spirits came, not the seal spirits of the Bladder Feast, but other spirits. Other people could not see or hear them but old men said they came.

6. Then the men went inside and painted dishes. Then they blew up the bladders and the Bladder Feast started. People wore all their best new clothes. All the women and girls, before the feast started, washed our hair outdoors even though the water froze to our hair. It was very cold.

7. I was afraid when the spirits came in the kazigi. Harmon was holding me and he reassured me. Harmon and his sister, Agana´-gachuNakh, Pearl's mother, are my cousins.

8. People took the seal bladders down to the holes in the ice, punctured them with little sticks, and put them under the ice. They sang songs and shook the little drums. After the Bladder Feast, they had a Patu´khtagalu´tiN.

9. One time Harmon (or was it Lewis?) and Russell came up to Nash Harbor to get people for a Messenger Feast at Cape Mendenhall. There were three wealthy men down there then: Simon, Aaron, and James Chani´ko´guyakh. As part of the feast, four of us older children raced: Ethan, A´giyakh (adopted daughter of Aaron), Gregory, and myself. Ethan was slow. Aaron told him to cry like a dog. He did and then he ran faster [laughter]. (Chani´ko´guyakh was the father of Dan Johnson, not real father—he had adopted Dan.)

10. These three wealthy men gave a lot of things. Aaron gave ten wolverine skins, ten big bearded seals, and many other things. Gregory's mother's father received so much he got rich. He was an old man, so he received the most.

11. Women and girls—we wore dance headdresses with reindeer hair and we danced. The fathers of the girls and the women's husbands did not give any presents for them, except fine food. Icha´-ganin, mother of Ezra and Rose, was a shaman. She drummed and showed her shaman-power at this feast. Before she became a shaman, she was very poor. After she became one, she married and got rich.

12. Simon used to be very wealthy. He had a wooden boat, in fact two. He bought them at St. Michael. Before he married Ada, he was married to Cha´kkakh and had a son.

13. I had an older sister, but she died.

14. At the time of that big feast at Cape Mendenhall, Harmon married Rose. Later they separated and he moved to Nash Harbor.

15. My family stayed at Ka´nigiakhtuli´gamiut a little while. The older sister of Celia and Catherine, named Na´nnokhka´Lagia, was sick. My mother went to see her every day. One day mother couldn't go, so she sent me to see how Celia's sister was. I went into her house alone. The sick woman scared me and I ran home to my mother. Mother went to see and found the sick woman dead. That was the first time I had seen a dead person.

16. They dressed the woman in new clothes, with a gut parka too. They took her out on the hill. My father cried. I wondered about this—it was the first time I had seen a man cry. I was about the size of Danny [she was about seven years old, younger than Danny]. My father was no close relation to Celia's sister, though they might have been cousins.

17. Na´nnokhka´Lagia had been married to Chu´qa. He was also married to Nako´gutaiLiNokh then. Na´nnokhka´Lagia had left him at Kani´khligamiut where he lived and went south to her family. Soon she got sick and died.

18. At that time, Akhsi´gakh was living with Ta´nnagikh and his wife: she was adopted. Dennis and Pantu´Nan also lived at Ka´-nigiakhtuli´gamiut, part of Ta´nnagikh's household. Victor [son of Dennis] was born while my family was staying there. At that time, when Harmon was still married to Rose, she did not have Oliver. Acha´khlukh was married to Gregory's grandfather then [and] they had adopted Oliver.

19. Lewis (my father's sister's son) and Masoa´lokh, son of Ta´nnagikh and brother of Pantu´Nan, were out in kayaks fishing one day when I and my mother were out picking celery. Masoa´lokh accidentally shot himself in the leg. I saw them bring him ashore. Just then a ship came. Three or four men and a woman in reindeer fawn parka came ashore. That was the first time I had seen such fur. (This was before the Lomen reindeer had been brought to Nunivak.) The white men and the woman opened Masoa´lokh's leg and removed the shot. But he died later.

20. They had come to get him because Naya´Ganiq when on trial in Nome had accused Masoa´lokh or implicated him somehow. But when they found Masoa´lokh hurt so badly, they left him. When he died, people wrapped him in a tent and took him out on a high place.

21. In this same period, we came north with Matthew, in Matthew's skin-boat, to Nuta´qamiut. Aaron also came. At that time, Matthew was married to A´giyakh. At Nuta´qamiut lived Stephen's father and mother. His father was named Kaowi´giyakh [Kaowa´-Gakh]. He was sick, he couldn't walk. His older sister, Ka´nnaGan, lived there and her five children.

22. We moved to Mekoryuk in Simon's wooden boat. We stopped at Kani´khligamiut on the way. I saw several people for the first time: Chu´qa and his sister, Joshua and his family, Asael's family, and Billy. Chu´qa's sister, Pantu´Nan, had three boys and two girls. The girls were much older. One of them, A´ganachi´akh, was married to Clarence Puguya´khtokh. (This was Luther Norton's family.)

23. Elizabeth's parents also came in a boat. Elizabeth's father, Ta´nnagikh, was a rich man and a shaman. He separated from Elizabeth's mother, IlaGa´Lagia, and married his son's widow, Ko´nakosiN. (That was Masoa´lokh's widow.)

24. My family came on from Kani´khligamiut to Mekoryuk. A´-qoaq's family lived here then. I saw Daniel's family for the first time: Chris and Nu´san, daughter of Amelia [Daniel's wife] by an earlier marriage.

25. We went on to Nash Harbor. Akha´LiNokh, who adopted Andy, was with us. Akha´LiNokh was not married then. Noah's grandfather, that was Austin's father, Kiawi´Gakh, was there. He was married to Rachel. When the boat came in toward Nash Harbor, men on the boat and on shore fired guns. I was scared.

26. Harmon had married Apu´Gan, Claudia's mother, after coming up to Nash Harbor [i.e., after separating from Rose]. Ernest's foster father, Anigi´lakh, and James Chani´ko´guyakh lived at Nash Harbor then. Anigi´lakh's adopted daughter, Helene, married Lewis while I was at Nash Harbor this time. Ta´nnagikh's family also came on to Nash Harbor.

27. When my father put out his seal net in the fall, he took me to the net with him.

28. At this time, James had adopted Theodore Uyu´kochi´akh and Martha. Theodore later was taken outside to a hospital and died.

29. This was the Bladder Feast at Nash Harbor: Anigi´lakh had one kazigi and James Chani´ko´guyakh had one. These people were in Anigi´lakh's kazigi [i.e., belonged to it]: Scott (my father), Lewis (Anigi´lakh's son-in-law), Awi´giyakh, and the boys. In James's kazigi were Harmon, Benson, Ta´nnagikh, and the boys. There used to be many people on Nunivak. Many have died.

30. The young men of the two kazigis raced to get celery. Lewis and Herbert Noga'takh tied. Theodore was second. Theodore—he was adopted by James—was angry because he didn't win and he broke the skylight of the rival kazigi, Anigi'lakh's kagizi. His father gave a new window. The Bladder Feast was held separately in the two kazigis. It was while the people were dancing and giving presents that the skylight was broken.

31. My family and I went on to a fish camp, Kaya'gayeli'gamiut. I saw a boy coming in a kayak, with a very dirty face. He was Kaya'Gakh, Jerome, brother of Ernest and Tu'ntukh. We had our supper across the river with Noga'takh's parents. I saw something, spirits or something, at the window. I also saw in one house a very old woman in a feather parka, Kaya'Gakh's grandmother. (Her nickname was Apa'Nuikaha'LiNokh.) The old woman was bent forward with her chest on her knees. She never moved. My parents went out to fish, but I said I was tired. I didn't fish; I played with Tumaga'niGaLagia, sister of Ernest. She put a live mouse in my parka.

32. We went back to Nash Harbor. I thought of the old woman as Bent Wōman. I asked my mother if her name was Bent Woman. Mother said yes. Later mother told father and he laughed. Then they told Anigi'lakh and his wife, and they all laughed a lot.

33. At that time, Anigi'lakh was married to Nuya'gayukh. Later she was married to U'mian and had a stepson, Luther.

34. Then my family, Anigi'lakh, and Benson's family went to Tachi'gamiut. Ernest Norton's father, Ta'olan, lived there. Also Kiogoyu'Gakh, of Bob's family. They got lots of seals in the spring. While I was playing one day, I saw Lewis's kayak tipped over by a piece of ice. He was unconscious. Ice fell on his kayak.

35. That was the first time I saw Bob's mother and father, and Andy's father, Akha'LiNokh. He was married to Constance then.

36. I remember something else about Ernest's and Jerome's grandmother. At the beginning of the summer, people removed the bearded seal blubber. When they finished that, they got mukluk [bearded seal] at Miksa'gamiut. My mother and Claudia's mother went to Miksa'gamiut, also Paul and myself. Claudia's mother was still married to Harmon then. That was the first time I had walked overland and the first time I saw Cape Mohican. It was calm clear weather. I saw mountains appear in the sea, with snow. I saw lots of white fox on the way to Miksa'gamiut. When we stopped to camp, we ran after the white fox, Claudia's mother with only one boot. We didn't catch any [laughter]. At Miksa'gamiut we slept only a little while. We got up to collect clams while the tide was out.

When we returned to shore, I slept a long time. When I woke up, my mother and Claudia's mother already had finished cutting the blubber of mukluk and spotted seal. Then they slept, too. While my mother and father were sleeping, I played with spotted seal intestine. It got dark for a while, in the afternoon. My parents woke up. Even though it was then evening and night, we walked back to Tachi'gamiut. It was an eclipse of the sun that I saw while playing. But I was not afraid.

37. I asked my mother about the old woman's name because my father had laughed. I didn't believe any more that her name was Bent Woman. My mother told me this was not her real name. Her real name was Awi'LaGan.

38. Some time later we were living at Talu'gamiut. I saw Tim Tutu'men's real parents there. We fished for salmon. Russell and Mani'Ganakh's father came from Cape Mendenhall to get my parents. We went back to Cape Mendenhall because Mani'Ganakh's father was my mother's father and wanted us to go. There were four kayaks: my mother, my father, Mani'Ganakh's father, and Russell. Our dog ran on shore. He swam across lagoons in order to keep up with us. When we came to U'chi'Nugamiut, a fish camp, we saw Russell's parents and Russell's children, three daughters and one son. While we waited there, my father and Russell went to Tachi'Nagamiut to get things that were stored there. I took a little boy, Fritz Russell, on top of the house. When I saw kayaks coming, I was happy, jumped up and knocked Fritz over. He rolled down off the house. When he cried, I was very scared [laughter].

39. Aaron came there. He brought IlaGa'Lagia, who had been married to Ta'nnagikh. Before he married her, his wife was Ila-Ga'Lagia's sister. She was pregnant; she got very big but the child was not born. She could hardly walk. Russell, Aaron, and my father stayed there and had a Bladder Feast even though only three men. I danced in the Bladder Feast for the first time. I recognized Russell from his boots and pants when he came in acting as the seal spirit. I was afraid of the spirits. To fight off the spirit, I grabbed his gut parka, nearly pulled it off, but he went out. He didn't come in again. At daybreak, we threw the bladders under the ice. I heard my father talking to the bladders, telling them to come back next year, but I did not understand what this meant.

40. There were small dances after the Bladder Feast. The women put soot on their faces in streaks. There were only a few people and not much happened after that. We stayed there all winter. In spring we moved to Cape Mendenhall. There was lots of hunting. Then they used the seal nets.

41. (Aaron later separated from his wife because of her big stomach. Mr. Bird, the first teacher, was here on Nunivak then. He tried to help, but she died.)

42. Then people removed the blubber of the mukluk.

43. Then we moved to U´chi´Nugamiut again. My grandfather was returning one day and found a big dead whale. All the people went to cut it up. They put the blubber and meat down in the ground. While they were cutting up the blubber, my mother's father got sick and died.

44. In the winter, people sent messengers to Kavalumiut. Nicholas and Ezra were the messengers. When people came for the feast at I´ta´gamiut at Cape Mendenhall, I saw Luther's family. One of the daughters, Miya´Gakh, had died. Luther's parents cried every morning, for their daughter.

45. Even though it was winter, people danced outside. Two shamans came out with big masks. One hollered like an animal. Most of I´ta´gamiut danced outdoors in the daytime. In the evening, the visitors danced. There were not many visitors. (Luther is younger than I.)

46. There was an epidemic. Many people were sick—they had colds. Many died. Austin's father Kiawi´Gakh and others died.

47. Zachary's wife at that time was a little woman from Nelson Island. Her mother was Naochia´Gakh. Her head always shook. When I first saw her, I thought she was feeling cold because her head shook. I asked my mother if the woman was cold; mother said the woman always had been cold. Then she died: she had a cold [influenza?] like the other people.

48. After that, Ermeloff [trader] came to Nunivak. I heard that reindeer had been brought. We had no dog chains. We had to wrap the dogs' muzzles so they wouldn't bite the reindeer. I was then about the age of Debbie Adam [i.e., about twelve years old].

49. Simon at that time had no wife: Cha´kkakh had died. He married ANa´Gakh even though she was quite young and small. Soon she had a baby.

50. Once, when I was small, I had an i´noGo tied on my belt. I didn't know what it was. When I got older, I looked at it and found it was a piece of fur seal skin and blubber. I threw it away. My mother made a rain parka for me and put a piece of sealskin on it, with something sewed inside. When I bit it, it made a noise. Some years later, I opened it and found little clam shells. I asked my mother what they were for. Mother didn't answer. So I threw the clam shells away. Before this, my parents wouldn't let me eat clams. When I was grown, one time I ate clams. I vomited

that night one clam, although I thought I had eaten a lot. After that, I ate clams and never vomited any more.

51. Mani ́Ganakh and his mother moved to Mekoryuk to live after his father died. Mani ́Ganakh's mother married IkhchuNai ́yakh, a brother of Asael Sharp. Dennis and Elizabeth lived at Cape Mendenhall. Aaron that winter married Nicholas's sister, ANi ́lan. When he moved to sealing camp, he left the woman with the big belly and took ANi ́lan. I was the same size as Debbie Adam then. I was married to Herbert Noga ́takh although I was small. I was afraid of Herbert. Whenever I saw him outside, I ran away and hid. He stayed in the kazigi, didn't come into our house. In the spring, Dennis and Elizabeth moved to Mekoryuk. In the summer, my family moved to fish camp, Herbert and I, too. But Herbert always slept in the storehouse. I still was afraid of him and ran away whenever I saw him. He went away and never came back. My mother asked me why I let him go—he might marry someone else. I was happy. He did marry someone else.

52. When I started to menstruate, I was put in a little hut. I was scared and ran away several times. I started to menstruate before I was married.

53. I wasn't married again because my father feared I might get more afraid of men.

54. After we went back to I ́ta ́gamiut, my father had rheumatism. He was very sick. All winter he never walked except with two canes.

55. Nicholas's stepfather, TaLi ́likh, was a shaman, also Ezra's mother, Icha ́ganin. She was called to heal my father. That was the first time I had seen a shaman try to cure. She covered my father with a rain parka. She sang, she began to tremble, her face got different. After she finished, she told him that TaLi ́likh had tried to kill him with his spirits; but that my father wouldn't die.

56. Aaron's son got sick and died in three days. Then the same night, at daybreak, Constance's brother died, too. Icha ́ganin told people that TaLi ́likh tried to kill my father but his bad spirit was turned away, to the children.

57. We moved to a fish camp named Nu ́naNana ́khmiut. My mother went to Nash Harbor to get Lewis. At that time, my father had a wooden boat. A week later, Lewis and his sister and my mother returned. We loaded dried fish and other things and moved to the north side of the island. On the way, it was fair weather. We stopped on the east side. A storm came up, so we stayed to pick berries. It was at Kani ́khligamiut—Chu ́qa and Chaki ́Lakh lived there. When it was calm, we moved on to Aki ́toq. We went on

toward Nash Harbor and met Iga lokh and Edwin Larson on the way. We arrived at Li´gakhmiut [Nash Harbor]. Then we lived there a long time.

58. My father got better. We stayed all summer.

59. Ernest and I went out in Mr. Bird's dory. Ernest couldn't row very well because it was so windy. (Ernest was younger than I.) I tried to take the oars from him and we had a fight. Ernest wouldn't let me have the oars. We nearly tipped the boat over when we wrestled for the oars. Ernest was younger but he was stronger. We had started out to get dry grass, but we went back.

60. Next spring we moved to Miksa´gamiut. (The name refers to the green slate used for points, etc.) While we were there, we ran out of food. My family tried to get food from Nash Harbor but got snow blindness. Mr. Bird put down in the record that I was eighteen years old at that time.

61. After we removed the blubber [i. e. , at the end of the spring seal hunt] Mr. Bird came with a boat to get us. Stephen and Helene came to Nash Harbor at the time that my family returned to Nash Harbor. Stephen and Helene had just been married. Bob's father died. Bob and his sister were small. There were Bob, Lillian Adolph, and Millicent. Stephen took Bob and Lillian. Millicent, who was taken by Joshua, died later. In the spring, Bob's mother and Lillian went with Stephen and his family to the south side. Stephen and Bob's mother were brother and sister. Bob's mother married Puguya khtokh. They had one child, Patrick Kapu´Gan.

62. When Patrick was about the size of Alfred, his mother died. Then Clarence Puguya khtokh married Pachu Niya.

63. I married Gregory at the time Patrick was born. Gregory came from I ta´gamiut to Nash Harbor by kayak. My family was living at Nash Harbor then. I was not afraid, I loved him right away. After that winter, Dorothy was born. I had no more children for three years; then Gilbert was born. We still were at Nash Harbor. Danny was born a year later; then Mildred, who died after Clarence Puguya khtokh died. My second Mildred was born in 1941. I had another girl at the time of the measles epidemic. The baby died immediately. I had no more children for two years, then Alfred, in 1944.

NOTES

2. Both Christine and her brother Paul recalled contests with their parents, in which they themselves usually won. They probably had such experiences more often than most Nunivak children, who go through periods of being negativistic, yet give the impression of being generally submissive. Apparently an open contest does not develop often.

4. Christine was vigorous, more alert and positive than most of the women. She might be called competitive, perhaps especially competitive toward men. She enjoyed recalling how she had beaten up her future husband. If he was the dominant member of the family, possibly she enjoyed "getting back at him."

6. Christine shuddered and shivered a little when recounting the hair-washing incident, evidently the first time she had gone through that ritual.

7. The recounting of family composition, bewildering to a reader, is due partly to Christine's individual interest, partly to a feminine concern with personal relations instead of the men's interest in relations with the external material world, and partly to my setting of the situation. In order to justify the request for these personal accounts, I said that I was interested in the villages and in life on Nunivak in past years, as well as in what had happened to the narrators individually. I asked in the beginning who had lived in the various settlements at different times and the family relationships.

9. Her laughing at Ethan seems to be further evidence of her competitiveness.

11. If this has been translated correctly, she danced in the Messenger Feast a few years before dancing in the Bladder Feast, mentioned specifically later. The latter occasion was more important. Icha´ganin was Daniel's first wife.

13. Christine needed little prompting. At this point, however, I asked whether she remembered the birth of Paul and how she had felt when he was born. She mentioned her sister but ignored the question regarding Paul. See her mother's autobiography for account of his birth. Christine may have been embarrassed by the circumstances of it although she need not have been. The sister, never otherwise mentioned, did not die during Christine's childhood but during early adulthood, after bearing two children. That Christine would tell of her whole childhood without mentioning her sister is remarkable.

15. Most of the Nunivak children of today observe death and the dead at an early age, even earlier than in Bernice's case.

17. Most of the autobiographies show the instability of the marital relations. Chu'qa was one of the few on the island in this period who had a polygamous household. It was obviously not a happy and stable one. Christine's parents seem to have been unusual in remaining together until the death of one of them.

18. Pantu'Nan was Ta'nnagikh's daughter. This shows the custom of a young couple living with the bride's family at least until after the birth of the first child, and occasionally much longer. Victor was the first-born of Dennis and Pantu'Nan (Elizabeth).

19. If Christine placed this correctly in the chronology of her childhood, then this event probably occurred in 1917. It seems likely, though, that she confused two separate events. The Naya'-Ganiq trial was in the early 1920's.

22. In this family peregrination covering three to four years, they progressed up the east side of the island, across the north and down the west side, living with various relatives or partners en route.

28. Going with her father to tend the seal net seems to have impressed her. While there was no tabu, men did not take young daughters on hunting expeditions as they would take sons. She probably was a favorite of her father.

31. The mouse prank evidently did not frighten her much.

32. Christine's facial expression may have reproduced her original feelings in the Bent Woman incident. It indicated that she was surprised, a little betrayed and resentful because her parents had laughed at what was a natural assumption for a child. She had believed her mother, then found her mother had deceived her. At the same time, she began to realize that she was naïve—that descriptive nicknames are not real names. This was part of the process of growing up for a Nunivak child. Formerly children never were told the real names of their elders. Thus probably they made their own assumptions regarding names, later being told the correct one, as in this case.

36. It is possible that she saw St. Matthew Island, not a mirage. Christine mentioned only one occasion on which she saw spirits. She either suppressed any account of visions and unusual spiritual experiences or else she had fewer than other Nunivakers.

This occurred June 8, 1918. The eclipse would have been seen from Nunivak Island at noon and early afternoon.

Being afraid or not being afraid was one of her chief interests in this account.

39. Christine must have been about nine years old when she first danced in the Bladder Feast. Others told of first recognizing the

true identity of the spirits in this way (i. e. , by fighting the spirit and in the scuffle finding out accidentally who he was).

41. As the Birds did not come until 1923-24, the woman must have had this condition (probably a large tumor) three or four years before her death. Christine resumed the narrative at 1919 after telling of her death.

43. Kin designations were not always translated and recorded in the speaker's exact terms, since the interpreter and I had the same fault: using the common designation of the person referred to. Possibly Christine did refer to her grandfather by the teknonymous term, "Mani´Ganakh's father," and to her maternal aunt as "Claudia's mother." There might be close feeling despite such formal designations. See paragraph 38.

46. This must have been in the summer of 1919, although to fit Christine's chronology relative to the eclipse, the only firm date that we have, it would have been 1920.

47. In telling of Zachary's mother-in-law and Ermeloff's coming to the island, she backtracked. The influenza epidemic and Mr. Ermeloff's bringing of the reindeer occurred before the arrival of Mr. Bird, first teacher. She went back to 1919 and even farther back to tell about her i´noGos; then resumed the narrative at 1922 or 1923. This dating fits with her statement that she was first married after puberty. She apparently was married at thirteen.

50. Christine's adolescence and young adulthood covered the period when the old belief in totemic powers was weakening.

51. Children knew the nature of sexual intercourse, and it is unlikely that normal Nunivak girls feared the sex act itself. But others as well as Christine told of resistance to an early, arranged marriage, and Daniel described the situation from the men's standpoint. Formerly, boys and girls from approximately six to thirteen kept apart from each other much more strictly than they do now. Girls lived apart from adult men even more. Hence there was a sense of strangeness that amounted even to fear. Moreover, it seems that in many cases the men were not tender or considerate and the girls had reason to be afraid. Most of the girls were childlike, dependent, unwilling to leave the relation of dependency on parents. They were given little chance to go through a normal adolescence, and rebelled against being forced into adulthood. Finally, there are indications that there was, anciently, greater hostility between males and females than there is now.

56. This shows how the great hostility toward a shaman might develop.

59. Ernest, serving as interpreter, said he had entirely forgotten the incident until Christine now reminded him of it.

60. Christine probably was sixteen or at the most seventeen,
not eighteen, years old.

63. Gregory and Christine were married in June, 1929, when
she was eighteen or nineteen years old, several years older than
most Nunivak girls at marriage and birth of the first child.

ZACHARY (CHRISTINE'S UNCLE)

Paul Scott, Interpreter

Zachary was the maternal uncle of Christine and Paul. Paul became interested in recording the family history. Also, he and his elders probably were glad to get the money that I paid for their time spent in telling me these personal stories. Paul brought first his uncle, then his mother a few days after Christine had told me about her childhood. Both Zachary and Nu´san needed much prompting and reassurance. They did not go ahead as if wound up, as Christine had done.

Zachary was slightly lame, not so crippled as Richard Chappel, however. In recent years he had earned his living chiefly by ivory carving, supplemented by some fishing and hunting with the assistance of an uncouth young man and his family who lived with Zachary and his wife. Apparently they always had been poor, unkempt, and unable to give as good care to their children as Christine's parents had been able to give. Zachary's carving was good in technique and showed considerable imagination and originality although not quite up to the highest standard of Nunivak work. Zachary seemed to be a pleasant, unobtrusive, hard-working man, a follower, not a leader.

As Paul had difficulty with tenses in English, the tenses have been made consistent in this translation and the grammar corrected.

1. My first memory: I was lying against my grandmother's breast. I thought she was my mother. She was eating caribou meat. But I don't remember seeing live caribou.

2. My next memory: it was summer and I was hunting birds with bow and arrow. I started early in the morning and I shot a ptarmi-

gan at noon. My parents gave a feast in honor of my first bird.

3. That same year, before winter, my family was fishing with a net at the mouth of the river. My parents threw the fish on the beach. I thought the fish were sandy, so I washed them. They carried the fish up to the house, and there I found a very big pile of fish. My family worked a long time cleaning them. Then my mother cooked some fresh fish, we ate, and I went to sleep.

4. The next spring, we were going to fish for cod. First we got flounders to bait the hooks. I went out with a man, not my father, to get cod and we caught lots. From then on, I remember all the time.

5. We lived at Nash Harbor then. That summer my father died, and that fall my mother died. I never had any brothers. I had two younger sisters; both of them are still living. But my father was not the father of the girls. My father was Tachi´Lka; their father was I´NaN. My mother was married two times. When my mother died, we children were separated. Ernest Norton's father took Apu´Gan (Claudia's mother); I´NaN, my stepfather, kept Nu´san, Paul's mother; and I´NaN's sister took me. Her name was Acha´-chakh.

6. I´NaN lived longer than my mother; he remarried and had Mani´Ganakh, Martha, and two other girls.

7. At Nash Harbor, when I was a boy, my own father was noga´L-piakh (wealthy man), boss of the kazigi. There was only one kazigi there then, a big one. Later a second kazigi, a smaller one, was built. I´NaN became boss of the big kazigi and my father was boss of the little one. When my father died, I´NaN was the big noga´Lpiakh.

8. After my father died, I´NaN made me a kayak, and I started to hunt the next spring. I hunted all spring and got only two ring seals. From the beginning, I used a gun for hunting, not spears.

9. I don't remember when I made my first song or when I got my first drum. As far back as I can remember, I used the drum.

10. In the old time, when a boy got the first of these five seals, mukluk, levtak, spotted seal, ring seal, and sea lion, he had to observe the tabus, for all the same as for mukluk.

11. When I caught my first mukluk and reached the shore, the old men told me to take off my pants even though it was cold and run to the village to get my sled. But I still was wearing my wooden hat and rain parka. When I got the sled, I put the seal on it and took it to the village. The men would not let me eat. While the people were sleeping that night, my mother took me to her store-

house and took off all my clothes. She painted my wrists and ankles and other joints with soot. I wondered about this. Then she put my clothes on me and took me back to the kazigi. She told my step-father to let me sit down but not to let me sleep all night. My mother took off all her ornaments that day, and I took out my ivory labrets and put in wooden plugs instead. I tried but I could not stay awake all night. Next morning I ate with the other men. I couldn't eat anything sweet or any fresh fish until after the Bladder Feast. And for five days in the Bladder Feast, I ate nothing. It was very hard for me when other people were eating in the kazigi. I was allowed to drink water and my mother put a little caribou fat in the water. I wondered at this because I never had seen caribou. My mother must have saved that tallow for a long time.

12. When I was a boy, a hunter's wife, or his mother, took the seal's bladder in the kazigi before the hunter ate. While the man blew up the bladder, the oldest man (who didn't hunt any more) used a small drum, only about seven to eight inches across, and sang songs belonging to the hunter's family, songs about bladders and hunting and spirits. Not the old man's own songs, but the hunter's family's songs.

13. I caught about five mukluk before I was married. In my whole life I have caught about twenty.

14. When I was a boy, people practiced new songs for the Bladder Feast, in the kazigi in the evening—without lights—for a month and a half or two months.

15. Sometimes, on the fifth night the wealthy men gave valuable presents: new kayaks, tents, and other expensive things. They were put in the kazigi, then divided by one man, who gave them to the old men and widows first. Then he gave presents to the next oldest and the next and so on until he gave presents to everybody. He gave clothing to the widows. The wealthy man divided up the things.

16. I was afraid of the spirits that came in the Bladder Feast. I didn't know really who they were until after I was married. Then the men told me to be the spirit. I was very surprised to find that the spirit was a man.

17. Regarding i´noGos, a man would have one, or three, or five. One man did not know how to use another man's i´noGo. I never wore the head of my i´noGo although some other men did.

18. When Paul was a boy, I married my wife, the wife I have now. My wife's uncle did not like me, he told her to refuse me [sexually]. She ran away to another village and hid. She sent a

message that I should follow her, but I didn't understand the message. Instead, I went to Nelson Island to get a wife. But my first wife and I got together again.

19. When I was first married, I was living at Cape Mendenhall. I was married in the autumn. My first wife never had been pregnant, she was barren until the bride feast. Then we had the bride feast. Only two months later, she ran away although she was pregnant then. She was carrying Judith Chris.

NOTES

1. It is hard to see just why Zachary described what must have been a common scene in his early childhood. It is possible that his mother rejected him wholly or partially, his grandmother taking the mother role, or perhaps some essential element—such as the grandmother denying the meat to him—was omitted.

3. His earliest memories are all in some way connected with food, obtaining and eating food. Aside from general oral interest, it is difficult to see why the little incident of the fish cleaning should have impressed him so strongly, as it evidently did. Perhaps his family laughed at him for washing the fish. Or it may have been that he had to wait too long for his supper, became hungry and frustrated. Perhaps the great pile of fish was reassuring to him in his food-anxiety.

4. This was a period of family conflict and anxiety because his father deserted his mother and him for another woman. See Nu´-san's statement. Zachary did not reveal that his father had deserted him, to explain why he went fishing with another man, not his father.

5. He did not mention his half sister by his father. He mentioned only his half sisters by his mother.

Zachary was proud of his father's position, but he obviously was identified emotionally with his stepfather, I´NaN, and with his stepfather's family, which adopted him. In the rivalry between his father and stepfather, he must have experienced emotional conflict, no matter how vigorously he identified himself with his stepfather. This is what happened, apparently: I´NaN bested Tachi´Lka in the economic race, assuming leadership of the kazigi at Nash Harbor. Then Tachi´Lka built a smaller kazigi of his own. As there were only four extended-families in the village at that time, according to Nu´san, neither man had a large following in his village although they probably had additional adherents in other villages.

9. When his talk lagged, to start him off again I suggested that he tell about the firsts in his life. These usually were exciting and happy memories for Nunivakers.

11. The woman whom he referred to as his mother was his foster mother. This passage shows how intimately he was related to his foster family and how completely he must have rejected his father's family or felt rejected by it. The latter supposition explains the interest in food, symbol of affection and nurture.

13. This is not a large number of mukluk (oogruk) caught, compared with the records of the best hunters.

14. He gave quickly at this point an outline of the essential elements of the Bladder Feast. As this has been recorded elsewhere several times, it is omitted here. He seemed to reveal nothing personal in the account.

16. Zachary was older than most Nunivakers when he learned the real identity of the spirits. This is an important revelation regarding his personality. He apparently was unaggressive, suggestible, and submissive to stronger people. Possibly, too, the older generation dared not resist the spirits and the directions of the old men as Paul's and Ernest's generation did.

18. He implied by tone that he did not want to understand his wife's message. It was several years before he remarried his first wife, who also had married another spouse in the meantime.

NU'SAN (CHRISTINE'S MOTHER)

Paul Scott, Interpreter

1. When I was a girl, there were only four houses and one kazigi at Nash Harbor: one man, Upa ́Guwakh, and his family—none is living now. One son of this man was Adolph Wilson's father, Ki ́-ogoyukh. This son was adopted by Tachi ́Lka's brother. Upa ́Guwakh and I ́Nan account for two households. Upa ́Guwakh was mother's-brother of my mother, A ́nman.

2. Tachi ́Lka's household was the third one. Tachi ́Lka left A ́nman, married another woman and was the father [by this woman] of Constance Ezra, Nu ́san.

3. Tim's mother's family was the fourth family.

4. Sailing vessels used to come. They sold tobacco and some food. Nunivakers liked to get tobacco. People on the ships did not buy furs, only carved ivory. At first, they wanted toothpicks, little ivory axes and spears, and ivory chains. Nunivakers did not buy coffee, tea, flour, or anything except tobacco and lead and powder. Nunivakers paid for them but the ships gave the food; people did not pay for it. Nunivakers were anxious to get matches too.

5. The first trader on the island was Lewis' father's father. He was a very strong, healthy man—a rich man.

6. After the sailing ships, one white trader came here sometimes to buy fox. Not many whites came to this island to trade, though. Not much trading with whites here. Nunivakers did trading on the mainland.

7. My father gave a Messenger Feast when I was a girl. He invited people from Mekoryuk, that is, he invited the chief of Mekoryuk. Any other people in the village who wanted to go could go along with the chief's family to the feast. My father, when he was getting ready for the feast, found a large whale and put it away for winter. In the fall, in the net he got lots of seals and white whales. He also got a lot of fish and he dried it. He never used

a dog team. He owned only two dogs. He put the dogs on the sled, one on each side of the sled, to haul the dried fish. No, this was not the time when my father found a whale when Christine was young. While I was growing up, my father found five big whales, and, before I can remember, he found many others. He was a rich man because he found so many whales. We never find them now. Sometimes he found big harpoons in the whales, from the whaling ships.

8. One time, when Paul was small, his grandfather found a dead whale, a very big one, that hadn't been dead long (the one Christine told about). We put the whale blubber in mud, a clay mud, to keep it from the flies. It did not get bad except a little on the outside of each piece. Inside, it stayed good for years. We used to keep it a long time. We dug a pit in the mud and put in the blubber. Water would come in the pit and freeze in the fall, and make like cold storage. Whale oil tastes very good. People usually didn't eat the meat unless it was one that had not been dead long.

9. At the end of the feast at Nash Harbor, then Mekoryuk people invited those people from Nash Harbor to come for a feast. They always had to return the invitation the same year.

10. The two games that children played most when I was a girl were amiGu'takh and malu'makh. Boys and girls played together. Girls skipped rope. All played a ball game [keepaway], starting when the first egg was found in the spring. One day when people heard that someone had found eggs—that usually was when we still were at seal camp—girls made a new ball. After supper, people played ball very happily. Everybody was glad that summer had come. Then they played ball all during the summer.

11. amiGu'takh was played on the beach. malu'makh was played in the winter. Children also played hide-and-seek in the long grass in the village.

12. I was married to another man before I married Na'nnoq. I was married in the fall and left my husband in late winter. I had no children from him. Then I married Na'nnoq. I was living at Miksa'gamiut when I married the first time. I was living at Kaya'-gayeli'gamiut when I married the second time. Christine was born at a camp at Cape Mendenhall. It's further out toward the cape than the winter village. Paul was born on the side of Robert Stone Mountain. We were on the way back to I'ta'gamiut from the Messenger Feast at Mekoryuk. We were traveling alone, with dogs—no other family. There was no woman to help. Na'nnoq helped me a little but not much. Paul rolled down on the snow when he was born. Na'nnoq put me on the sled and took me on home to the village.

NOTES

1. I asked her specific questions to fill in gaps and explain statements made by her brother Zachary, but without always indicating the exact purpose of my question. To understand better the rivalry between her father, I῀NaN, and Tachi῀Lka, I asked who lived in Nash Harbor when she was a girl. She would answer my questions but volunteered little of the comment that I hoped for.

4. Because of Zachary's fine, wavy hair, I suspected that his father was a white man, hence asked about white traders. Nu῀san did not tell what Daniel and others told, so I proceeded to a question about her father's feast-giving.

5. The rich man referred to as grandfather of Lewis was also the father of Nu῀san's late husband, Na῀nnoq. She probably was both avoiding use of her husband's name and stating delicately the high position of her husband's family.

7. Paul, in interpreting, interrupted to comment: "Very different now." Paul used nine dogs and always rode on the sled. Condescendingly he repeated that his grandfather had to push the sled, with the help of only two dogs. Like young people elsewhere, most of the younger Nunivakers do not look back to the old days with envy or yearning.

10. This question regarding games was asked in order to get the relations between boys and girls. Her answers were so generalized and noncommittal that I decided not to continue with the questioning that was originally intended.

12. I had noted on a previous visit to Nunivak that she and her husband demonstrated their affection for each other more than most people of their age. They had seemed unusually happy together. I found on this visit that her husband, Na῀nnoq, was dead and that she had married the Eskimo missionary from the mainland and apparently was getting along well with him. I thought she probably had recovered from the loss of Na῀nnoq by now sufficiently to tell of her marriage to him, the birth of her children, and her early life with him; hence I asked her direct personal questions, having gotten so little response to impersonal ones. She talked willingly enough, but the experience was disturbing. She cried quietly and became embarrassed for having started to cry. Therefore, I expressed sympathy and ended the interview.

Zachary and Nu῀san, although half-siblings, had had a quite different start in life. Zachary's father lost in the economic competition and behaved badly. Nu῀san's father was a big feast-giver and accepted his community responsibilities.

PAUL SCOTT (CHRISTINE'S BROTHER)

In her autobiography, Christine mentioned her younger brother Paul but did not relate any experiences shared with him or tell of anything that happened to him specifically. Until recently brothers and sisters were kept apart from each other. Even so, Christine's account is unusually self-centered. She evidently was allowed to act with much more self-direction, independence, and self-concern than is allowed most young girls on Nunivak Island.

Paul in some ways was a better socialized person, less aggressive and more generous; yet he was more concerned with his own emotions than those of his children. He was quite conscious of his need to maintain his father's position as a prosperous man. Paul spoke English, although not well, and knew a little about modern business methods. He was manager of the community store for two or three years, not doing especially well in the position because of his ignorance of bookkeeping rather than any dishonesty or bad judgment.

He seemed not to have loved his first wife, who died, quite so much as he did his second, an unusually dependent person. This wife had not yet grown up, but she probably was emotionally responsive to Paul in a young-girl manner. Paul's love for the children she had borne him also was great. She had been married before, to Daniel's son who died. This was mentioned in Daniel's account.

Paul's maternal aunt and her son and daughter lived with him at this time, doing much of the routine work of the household. His two eldest children, by his first wife, also did a child's full share of work.

Paul served as my interpreter occasionally, a willing one but not so good as Ernest Norton or Duncan Cook because of his poorer knowledge of English. The following incidents were related in Eng-

lish at different times and not in chronological order. While I have
tried to preserve his personal idiom as much as possible, the
circumstances did not always permit recording the wording exactly.
Perhaps we would be standing on the beach, watching the children
playing, when he would relate one of these little stories.

1. I remember my mother make me a bird skin parka. I was same size as my boy, maybe I'm three years old then. She made it from skins of bird that looks like puffin, but half of its breast is white and half is black. We call that bird akha ´Ni ´aGakh and we call the parka made from that bird akha ´Ni ´aGat. I don't like that parka and I don't want to wear it. I cried hard as I could but my mother make me wear it. When I'm playing outdoors, I took it off. My mother saw me, she see that I don't have that parka on, and she put it on me again. Then I look until I find a little hole in it—just a little hole—and I put my finger in it. I tore it and tore it until I rip it nearly whole length of it. My mother don't say anything, she just sew it up and put it on me again. Then I hunt for something to make it dirty. I rolled that parka around in ashes and I stuff it in a hole.

2. I think maybe my mother tell my father and I'm afraid of what he say, so I go where he is, to see if he says anything. My father never say anything about that parka. And I don't say anything about it. Then I went to my mother but she never say anything, either. She never try to make me wear that parka again.

3. I often think about this since I'm grown; I wonder why I don't like that parka so much. I think maybe this is reason: I been wearing parkas made of squirrel and puppy, and other soft things. Bird skin parka is rough and heavy—it scratches. I think that's why I don't like it.

4. When I was a little boy, I had a dish made like an animal. My grandfather make it for me. One day I eat down by shore of the lake. When I finish, I put a mast and a sail on my dish, and I sent it out on the lake. But it won't come back. I can't get it. Long time after that, many weeks or many months, my parents found my dish on other side of the lake—long ways. They don't punish me because I lost that dish.

5. In the Bladder Feast, they gave Mani ´Ganakh and me to spirit at same time, Mani ´Ganakh and me, together. He grabbed our legs and held us on the ground [i. e., floor of the kazigi]. But he don't hold both my legs—he get hold of only one leg. With my other leg,

I kick him in the head. He went out and he don't come back. I go out and I see Russell's nose was bleeding. I know then he was the spirit. After that, people don't give me to the spirits any more. I was only five years old.

6. When I was a little boy, my father put a wolf's head on my head in Bladder Feast. I didn't know why he put it on.

7. The first year I go out hunting in kayak, all I get is a little ring seal. My father won't let me eat anything sweet until after next Bladder Feast, but he let me eat fish, and he won't let me eat anything for three days in the feast. I don't get weak, I don't dream anything while I'm not eat. Some boys who were not healthy—they get weak when they don't eat.

8. When I was naughty, when I don't do what my sister or my mother tell me, my mother told me that spirits get me. That was the only thing that make me be good. I was really afraid of spirits. People scared children by telling them about spirits and made them behave. They did good.

9. They never paint me—like Zachary told about—when I got my first mukluk. But they told me to stay awake all night. I couldn't do it. I went to sleep.

10. My father tell me when I was a young boy that I don't need to eat women's food and if they give me something to eat in those other houses, I do not need to eat that food, but I must not waste it. One time, Adam's mother (she was a "sister" to my mother) she gave me some dried food (some fish or meat) in her house. I took it but I throw it away when I went outside. I went home and told my mother I throw it away. She scolded me—she said I should never throw away any food.

11. When I was little, I used to play outside all day. Sometimes I go out to play in the morning and I don't come back until it's evening. I never think of hunger. Then in the evening I'm too tired to eat. I eat just a little and then I crawl under the covers and go to sleep with my boots on. Later my mother wake me up and take off my boots, but she never scold me. Or maybe if I have something to eat during the day, I don't eat anything at night when I'm tired from playing. I play *all* day.

12. When I was about Danny's age [nine or ten years old] my father and mother told me and Christine to get some small fish in the river. We went alone, just two of us. That was on the south side of Nunivak. I was walking down river and I spear the fish as I go. I look at the fish and I don't notice where I go and I walk into a place where my feet can't touch bottom. I yelled to Christine that it was too deep. I went on, walking in the water even though

Figure 2. One type of boy's dish—this one worn from use—showing family design in bowl and seal form of dish, which individualize it. (See Lantis, 1946, p. 190, Fig. 33, for another type of dish for a boy.)

I don't touch the bottom. I still go down the river—I don't try to get out. And Christine—she was running along on shore beside me. Just when my duck parka get all wet and begin to feel heavy, I touched bottom and I walked out. Then Christine and I, we were both crying when I got on shore. Christine wasn't hurt at all but she cried as hard as I did. We both worry about my wet parka. I think we were crying about that.

13. When I was a boy, I don't like fresh codfish or fresh flounders, but I'm *very* fond of salmon and trout and seal meat. Sometimes I didn't eat because I didn't like the food. My mother didn't say much about it. But she didn't give me anything else. Next meal she gave me same food I had before. She saved it. But I wouldn't eat it. Then I'd get very hungry and I'd eat it—same food. She'd give it to me two, three times, until I'd get so hungry I'd eat it.

14. Benson made me my first kayak. Benson was a very good carver. He is my father's nephew. I don't know how it was, but my father always called Benson his nephew.

15. Three years ago, Lewis and Ted Cook and I were out in our kayaks: we hunt seals. It was in March. I was at Nash Harbor that time—we went out from there. There was heavy fog. I don't know

how far out we went in fog. Then the fog went away and a storm
came, a southeast wind. That's an offshore wind over there. It
blew us way out, away from Nunivak. Probably we're twenty to
twenty-five miles out, but we didn't know it. I got one mukluk and
Lewis got two. We started to come back and we have to paddle
against the wind. We nearly lost the ice [i.e., the wind was blowing
the ice away, offshore, so that they did not have the protection
of the ice; they could not paddle in the lee of it]. We have no wind-
break then. The wind is getting stronger. I tow Ted's kayak. After
while, Lewis can't go much longer. Lewis get too tired, so I tell
Ted I have to let him go and maybe he can go to shore by himself.
We were about ten miles out then, I guess. Ted went on—he make
it all right. He come to shore over west of Nash Harbor. Then I
tow Lewis clear in to Nash Harbor.

16. I'm not afraid for myself, that time. I know I can get to
shore. But I'm very afraid for Lewis and Ted. I think they can't
make it. The kayaks go all right, they're not too heavy.

17. Richard Ka´Nalikh's brothers were drowned at sea, on the
south side, both at the same time. The body of one of his brothers
washed ashore, but not the other one.

18. Ted Cook was lost this summer. There was very great calm
for two days when he went out. He went alone. Then a storm came.
Nobody ever found him.

19. I nurse [nourish, take care of] seven. Christine and I have
more children than any other family. I have my wife Anne, Anne's
boy (Harold); Thomas and Leila (Lagau´taGakh's children), Walter, Raymond's mother and Raymond's sister. Raymond's old
enough to take care of himself.

20. Anne had two children—she gave one away to her sister. I
had three children with Lagau´taGakh. Asael Sharps [her father
and mother] take one girl, Melissa. She's their granddaughter.
Melissa do better with me. I don't know—they don't seem know
how to take care of her.

21. Walter's my boy. He always play alone. He take care of
himself. We name the baby [born two nights previously] Na´nnoq—
English name, John—for Anne's father, and my father's name,
too. She begin to have pains in evening, baby come about 3:30 in
morning. I help her, I take the baby, and Raymond's mother wrap
it. Anne don't have bad time—she fine now.

22. Children all with me, I take care of them, even Anne's in
bed.

23. [In answer to questions:] Walter likes the baby fine. He's

weaned long time now. He never suck now, just drink milk. He likes milk, sugar, and berries best. Walter's fat and healthy. He don't learn to walk like my other children: he's slower to learn. Thomas, he learn to walk quick: he was born in November and next September he can walk, holding on to things, and in October he walk alone.

24. [Paul saw Melissa nearby.] Melissa think Asael and Alberta are her father and mother. I tell her I'm her father but she won't believe me. I want her to know I'm her father and that I like to have her, because I think maybe her grandpa or grandma die or maybe both die soon, then I'll take her back. Then she will come to me [i. e., will be emotionally prepared to come]. I think Asael and Alberta don't take good care of her. I don't like that.

25. Melissa's four and a half years old now. I gave her to Asael and Alberta when she's one and a half years old.

26. Last winter I trapped only two weeks and got nineteen white fox. Some people trapped longer, got only ten, twelve. Some years I catch forty fox, if I trap all season and it's a good year. Last year I trap alone but I gave half my traps to Raymond [parallel cousin, member of his household] and I let him take my team. Raymond set out other line, he follow his own line.

27. Raymond hunted in kayak before this year but he don't get anything until this spring. He do O. K. this year: filled his kayak with seals every time. He catch ring seal and spotted seal, and levtak too. I took skins and oil to Bethel to trade, Raymond's too. I got twenty-five dollars for a poke, about ten gallons of oil. Some people got thirty-five dollars for big pokes. I got thirty dollars for a mukluk skin [for each skin].

28. Last year when I was trapping, I was caught in a bad storm. I was way over in the middle of Nunivak. The first day I was out— before the storm—I got five white fox. Then I went over on west side of some hills to rest and get shelter for my dogs. Storm came up, so I make camp. Then next day I start back along my trap line but I don't find my traps. Very bad storm: I can see only eight to ten feet ahead of me. I walk along, and I look at my compass. But I can't go far. So I make camp behind those hills. While I'm in camp, waiting for that storm to end, I run out of food. I have no food for my dogs or for me. Then one evening it is a little clearer. I come over those hills and for just a little while I can see the Reindeer Hills over here, not far from Mekoryuk. Then I know which way to travel. So I watch my compass and I can find my way home (to Mekoryuk) even though the storm get bad again right

away and I don't see anything. When I got home, people were worried. Other boys were out, too, but they all came home. I was only one out in the island. I had no food for three days.

29. I love Walter *very* much because I love Anne. I can say to Walter, "I love Walter," and I can say to Leila, "I love Leila," but I can't tell Thomas that I love him. I love Thomas, but not like Walter and Leila. Leila is my only girl now, only girl I have in my house, so I care for her more. Thomas won't work with his hands. When I'm a boy, I'm always carving and making things like my father make, but Thomas don't do this.

30. Walter is strong, he's very healthy. He learned to walk when he's young. Thomas learned to walk and to talk when he's very young, too. Walter always like to play by himself. He just goes by himself.

31. I nurse nine people. I have big burden, but I like to take care of my children. Melissa's grandparents don't do right with her. I don't like it but I don't say anything. I give Melissa clothes sometimes, but she's dirty and maybe they don't feed her enough. I like to take her, but maybe they don't live long and then I'll take Melissa.

NOTES

1. Paul probably was older than three years, indicated by the purposefulness of his behavior and the clarity of his memory of the incident. In any case, this happened about thirty years before.

2. He was not so shrewd or not so frank in analyzing his and others' motivations as were some other Nunivakers. In this incident, he was in a contest with his mother. This was shown by the increasing determination in his voice as his recital progressed. He finally won, but wasn't at all happy at having defied his mother and won. He probably was a less defiant boy, or at least less openly defiant, thereafter. He felt guilty and wanted his parents to punish him, to expiate his guilt. So he sought them out, hoping they'd punish him. But they didn't.

3. The black and white of the parka, as well as its harshness, may have affected him initially, before the matter became a contest of will, or it may have had some meaning that he was not aware of.

4. I asked whether his parents punished him in any way for losing the dish. Evidently they all thought it quite remarkable and amusing that his dish sailed clear across the lake and was found, and he remembers the incident because of this fact principally rather than his guilt for having lost the dish.

5. Paul told his own experience in learning about the Bladder Feast spirits after he heard his uncle's account (see page 45). He was pleased with himself for having resisted and found out the real identity of the spirits when he was only five or six years old.

6. The autobiographical material from others besides Paul indicates that children went through ritual acts and wore regalia as directed for several years, perhaps through their entire childhood, before being told the meaning of these things. The wolf head represented his family's principal totem.

7. Paul had to fast only three days while his uncle had had to fast five days. This may show a decline in the enforcement of old custom. Or perhaps Paul was younger than many of the boys when he caught his first mukluk. Or, more likely, his father was more indulgent.

I had asked how he felt when he didn't eat, and whether he had any special dreams. Paul boasted: he always presented himself as stronger than others. And he did not laugh at himself or at others so easily as Christine did. He may have been a bit anxious and sensitive at this time, needing to reassure himself, because of a community disagreement over his erstwhile management of the store.

8. When he said, "They did good," he meant that good was accomplished by means of the spirits. He was excusing and justifying the old Nunivak belief. He was defensive, as suggested by the boasting and other traits.

11. He always presented his mother favorably, spoke of her with pride. He told surprisingly little about his father, especially as a boy normally was reared chiefly by his father. Yet other accounts and observations confirm that a boy and his mother (or elder sister or other mother-substitute) felt very close to each other.

12. Again, he didn't admit fear. He had said that he was afraid only of the spirits.

15. Paul presented himself more than once as a helper and protector of others. This was partly conventional, as well-to-do men were supposed to help others. It also satisfied his need to appear big, strong, unafraid, not only self-reliant but even a father figure to others. Because of his father's death in recent years, he may have been more or less consciously taking his father's place.

Regarding Paul's statement that he was towing Ted: the latter was paddling, but Paul had a tow-line on his kayak to help guide and steady the young fellow's kayak. Lewis was older and a good kayak-man, but needed the strength of a younger man.

I asked whether he had prayed to his ki'Lka or to the Christian God when he was in such a dangerous situation. He looked surprised, laughed a little, said nothing. I asked then how he felt, whether he thought he might be lost at sea. He claimed that honestly he had not feared for himself. Paul was short but appeared to have strong shoulders for paddling, and his self-assurance was justified. He had met the threat in a forthright, practical, physical manner.

16. A mukluk (oogruk) being a large animal, I asked whether the carcasses plus all the hunting gear made a heavy load and made management of the kayaks difficult. I wondered whether a hunter in extremity would abandon a mukluk carcass, which is a great prize. Apparently it had not occurred to the men to throw out the animals and they undoubtedly were right. Kayaks ride better when heavily loaded. Also, shifting the load would have been a hazardous maneuver.

19. Paul had actually nine dependents, including the new infant and his cousin, Raymond, who was partially dependent on him.

20. Anne gave the child to her elder foster sister, her foster

parents' daughter. Paul grinned all the time he discussed Melissa, giving the superficial impression that he was more proud of his ability to care for her than concerned about her welfare for her own sake.

21. Walter, three years, usually did play alone, not because he could not get along with other children but because he had adequate means of amusing himself. During this conversation, although three other small children played near us, Walter played entirely by himself. Occasionally he did what they did, but not with them. He chuffed like a reindeer fawn as he ran around. He threw sand on a pup's face but did not maul it and showed little meanness. His fur clothing was fancily decorated and in good condition. Paul was very proud of him.

22. Paul's aunt, Raymond's mother, probably helped more than he said, especially in caring for the other children.

23. Walter was a plump, sturdy boy, as Paul said. He probably was slower in learning to walk because he was heavier than the other children.

24. Paul called Melissa to us and asked, "Who's your father?" She looked at him with an expression that seemed to be a combination of uncertainty, resentment, and resistance. She said nothing, frowned, and turned half away from him, but she remained near, still with the same expression. Apparently he felt that there was nothing that he could do or wanted to do.

25. Melissa was nearly six years old. She probably had been adopted when eighteen to twenty-four months old, as her mother had died when she was about one and a half years old.

26. Paul's statement was true: others said that trapping had been poor the preceding winter.

Raymond was eighteen years old, a good worker, but like any Nunivak boy without a father, he was dependent upon a well-to-do relative, in this case his "brother." Paul may have exaggerated Raymond's accomplishments because the boy's mother was listening.

27. I did not ascertain whether he gave cash to Raymond and his mother or whether he used their share of the money to buy things for them. A man disposing of his own son's products ordinarily would use the money in any way he thought best.

29. This was not said in Thomas' hearing. Nevertheless, Thomas knew Paul's attitude. On this occasion, Paul sent Thomas on three different errands in quick succession. At the third request, Thomas said "AW!" and acted quite irritated, but he went. He often acted resentful and hostile, yet in a quiet way. All of Paul's

children behaved in a subdued, self-contained way although they did not seem to be cowed and frightened. Paul, his aunt, or someone else in his household must have been a disciplinarian, but I did not find out how the discipline was effected. It may have been done by appeal to pride of family, by shaming and teasing, or by granting and withholding affection. If affection was withheld permanently from Thomas, he would not be responsive and obedient as Leila was (he had nothing to work for) and would become more disturbed than he was at this time.

Paul did not mention his stepson Harold; yet when I praised Harold's performance in a school program, Paul was interested and very proud. He grinned broadly.

31. He told the teacher that he wanted his wife, Anne, to go to the hospital even though she was not very sick. (She was recovering slowly from delivery.) He did not want Anne to die, he didn't want to lose her. As Anne was accustomed to being babied, this attitude satisfied both her needs and Paul's.

Paul's statement shows that children were not given for adoption with the unconcern and lack of subsequent interest in the child that observers often assume in Eskimo behavior. But the anxiety to get along with others in the community and the respect for one's elders were stronger than the parental concern.

THREE MEN WHO WERE NOT PROSPEROUS

THREE MEN WHO WALKED AROUND

EDWIN LARSON

Ernest Norton, Interpreter

Edwin Larson was a universally respected old man, said to be seventy years old or older, but probably nearer sixty-five. He was kindly, hard-working, and absolutely honest. His wife, however, was not so well liked, probably an extension to her of the old prejudice against her mother, who lived until after 1940, a very old lady and senile. Edwin never had been an outstanding hunter and wealthy man like his half brother, Matthew Larson, and he had only one young son to help him (son of his first wife, now dead). Further, this lad, a quiet, likable boy, was sent to a Government boarding school, leaving the old couple alone. They lived principally on fish, greens, and reindeer meat because Edwin could not hunt seals so vigorously now.

He revealed almost nothing of his early personal relationships. His account is interesting chiefly for its information on Nunivak life in the early historical period of the island. As Edwin lived on the east and southeast side of the island while Daniel was living on the west side, the former's account supplements the latter.

1. I lived at Cape Mendenhall when I was a little boy. There were two big villages then.

2. There was plenty of sunshine one day. I went up a hill: I was afraid but I don't know what I was afraid of. I was alone. I went to the other village and saw many people at the back of the village, dancing outdoors. These people outside the village were from Nelson Island. I forgot everything else while I was watching them. Next thing I remembered, I was in the kazigi, a big kazigi. I was sitting on my mother's lap, leaning against her breast. I could see clearly the people dancing. I saw some man come in wearing

white men's clothes and glass snow-goggles. The man hollered something, like this: "While I was poor, I was ashamed. Men were treading on me." This man was a wealthy person, named Aya´gina´Gakh, from Nelson Island. My father took the glasses and gave them to me. I kept them and when I was a young man, used them in seal hunting, but I lost them in the sea.

3. We used to have the Messenger Feast with Nelson Island people: they were invited here and we went over there rather often.

4. Then I forgot.

5. Then, in the winter village, I saw Nagokigina´gamiut people—they had a ceremony there. I remember people getting ready for the dance but I don't remember the dance itself. I slept, I woke up, finding my uncle sleeping beside me. He was named Ka´Nalikh. Many people were sleeping in the kazigi. Someone came in, in the early morning, wearing a squirrel cap, different from the Nunivak cap. The man stood on the kazigi floor with a cane. Someone awoke and said to the others, "Here's a messenger." Everyone woke up and welcomed him. A´nakhta´khnoakh was the messenger, from Nelson Island. The people went to the other kazigi then. A´nakhta´khnoakh was a relative of my ancestors.

6. After that I remembered everything.

7. My family got ready to leave Chikogali´gamiut at Cape Mendenhall. The sun was shining, there was a west wind in the morning. Many kayaks and three umiaks were leaving. We sailed across the harbor [bay], sometimes using oars. Many people from that village went to Nelson Island. We stopped at Cape Manning on the way. We sailed the next day. We slept at Nuta´qamiut, on a little island; next day we sailed to Nelson Island and many people from Nuta´qamiut, too. It was very calm and the sun was shining. That was my first visit to Nelson Island. We stopped on the south side of the island. Russell and I were playing. A storm came up, a heavy storm.

8. Then we went to Um´kamiut, where only two families were living. In the next village, there were many people. The man named A´nakhta´khnoakh took me in his house. They had good water from a stream. There were two kazigis there. Mainland people also came—Chafa´gamiut people, from south of Nelson Island. I remember everything of that ceremony; I remember the things they brought, but I don't tell what they were because there were so many things. Then we came home. From then on, I knew some Nelson Islanders. That is all I know about my childhood.

9. Some man named Chagu´milukh brought a wolf skin. Tunnaguga´lukh brought a wolverine. Kia´suq brought five guns. One man

from the Kuskokwim brought a boat sail or a tent. Many brought skins—oogruk and so on. Kila Nakh brought seven levtaks. These were all Nelson Island or Mainland people.

10. For the Messenger Feast, they had the same kind of dances, songs, and masks at Nelson Island as at Nunivak. In the ceremony, shamans performed. I was still a young boy. I had no brothers or sisters at that time. I was not old enough yet to use the drum. Later I had many brothers and sisters but they are all dead now.

11. That is all I remember about when I was a boy.

12. When I was a young man, I went to St. Michael several times. It was a big town then, had lots of people. Later, I went to the Kuskokwim.

13. No one taught me to hunt. I just followed one man and another—I learned by myself.

14. Once I saw a shaman dance and move around in the kazigi, holding his hands to his forehead, with his elbows out at the side, flapping them up and down. I did not understand what kind of being he was showing. One time Luther Norton and I were out hunting in kayaks. We saw something like a man come up and dance in the water and flap his arms just like the shaman had done. Then I understood. This spirit sank down and a seal arose in exactly the same place. Although I tried to shoot it, I couldn't hit it. I hadn't tried to shoot the spirit—I was afraid of it. Even though I was a grown man, I was very frightened. That spirit was not gono'nikh, the woman with long hair, who also sends up a seal or turns into a seal.

15. No, I do not remember any time when Nunivak people had no food.

16. I found out that the seal spirits in the Bladder Feast were a man when I was just a little boy—I discovered it from his clothing.

COMMENTS

Edwin Larson's own mother lived to old age. When she died in the winter of 1940-41, she must have been in her eighties, judged by the ages of her children. She was the only person on the island with entirely white hair; yet she was in remarkably good condition, able to do a little work in scraping and rubbing skins to soften them and able to get out and walk around with the aid of a cane, although going in and out of the underground house required some agility. She lived in Matthew's household.

Edwin Larson in his small, poor, dark house (in 1940), with his fat, slow-moving wife, dirty son, and mother-in-law who was a decrepit old crone, lived in very different circumstances from both his younger stepsister and stepbrother. He must have felt his poverty keenly although no one held it against him. On the other hand, he was admired. That he told only about the Messenger Feasts of his childhood is significant. In them, children saw wealth displayed and formed their resolutions also to be wealthy and admired. Edwin may have felt that he had a lifelong frustration.

NOTES

2. This first episode must have occurred in the 1880's or beginning of the 1890's.

9. From here on, most information was given in answer to my questions; for example, he was asked about the gifts to which he had referred.

12. These visits probably were made in the period between the Gold Rush and 1910. It is interesting that St. Michael, which was then a very bustling town, did not seem to impress the Nunivakers. They probably did not see or understand most of what went on there.

13. This statement explains why Edwin refused to talk about his youth although he was willing to talk about shamanism and other subjects. He did not seem to be afraid that I might ridicule or disbelieve. His father had died in Edwin's adolescence and his mother married Kusau´yakh and by him bore Matthew Larson and a daughter. Edwin, as the eldest child of the family, apparently was not adopted. He was cut loose to take care of himself, he was more or less alone, and poor. He must have been unhappy, or ashamed of his life in that period, hence would not or could not talk about it. For example, he did not answer my question as to who made his first kayak. He said only that he taught himself to hunt and then went on to tell about the seal spirit. His quoting, from his earliest memory, the man who said he had been poor and ashamed therefore becomes significant.

14. The experience with the seal spirit could not have happened more than fifteen to twenty years previously because Luther would not have been old enough to hunt before that. Thus Edwin was in his late forties or fifties. This explains the emphasis of his statement that even though he was grown, he was afraid.

15. Ernest Norton also said that there never had been starvation in the lifetime of anyone then living, although there were stories that long ago people did starve on Nunivak Island.

16. This was given of course in answer to my question. Having noted that the speed with which children discovered the true identity of the Bladder Feast spirits was generally diagnostic of independence or dependence and submission, I asked this question of most people.

LUTHER NORTON

Charlie Sharp, Interpreter

Although only thirty-six or thirty-eight years old, Luther seemed to belong to an older generation. For one thing, he was married to a woman much older than he who had been his stepmother when he was a young man. Second, he liked to carve masks in the old style and at the moment probably was the best carver of masks on the island. He knew more about the old belief and ritual than many laymen, especially the young men.

He was an unaggressive person—might be called sweet-tempered and apologetic. He snuffled and breathed as if he had adenoids and his eyes often were watery. Sometimes he looked as though he had a bad headache but he claimed that he was well. He and his wife and young adopted daughter gave every evidence of being quite poor: his dogs were unusually gaunt, his foster daughter was ill-kept. Yet, the preceding spring he had been one of the most successful hunters in catching oogruk.

1. I was born at Kani'khligamiut on the east side of Nunivak, not far from Mekoryuk and Cape Etolin, and I lived there while I was a little boy. The other families there were Daniel's family, Joshua [and his parental family], and Asael's family. We had moved to Naga'Gamiut by the time I was eleven or twelve years old, so everything that happened to me at Kani'khligamiut happened when I was under ten years old.

2. I liked to play in kayaks and go out in a kayak, and play with a model umiak. My playmates were Chris Daniel and Duncan U'mian.

3. I could spear salmon and kill small birds with bow and arrow. Boys don't spear salmon any more. When I was a boy, people used a bow very well—they got lots of birds. We didn't know

the law then; we didn't know that we should not kill small birds.

4. One time Stephen Ta'nnagikh and Ka'zigi'a, father of Rob, came as messengers from Ka'nigiakhtuli'gamiut to invite people to a Messenger Feast. Every family went from Kani'khligamiut and one family from Mekoryuk. Kakia'nakh was a wealthy man, very wealthy and strong: he was the principal feast-giver at Ka'-nigiakhtuli'gamiut. That was the first time I had seen people wear wooden masks at a dance. It was a big feast—several different masks and dances. People traveled [to the festival] with dog teams.

5. Another time, Nicholas and Ezra came as messengers from I'ta'gamiut (at Cape Mendenhall), inviting people to a Messenger Feast. People from Kani'khligamiut and a couple of families (not all families) from Kani'khligamiut went to the Feast. That was the first time I had been at Cape Mendenhall. They gave the Feast a little differently: they danced outdoors, gave things away outdoors, then went inside.

6. The first little bird I caught, my family dried the skin, hung it in the kazigi. They gave food to the older men and my father gave sealskins.

7. A big event was when I made my first song and sang it with my drum in the kazigi. I was about eleven years old. We lived at Naga'Gamiut then. My older brother gave a levtak, in honor of the song, to Edwin Larson's wife. She was not a close relative, but a cousin. When I caught my first mukluk, it was given to Edwin Larson. Then, the only families at Naga'Gamiut were Edwin Larson, Tim Tutu'men's mother, and my family. My father and mother were still living. My family sometimes lived part of the year at Nash Harbor.

8. My family was big: five boys and three girls. I was the youngest. Two boys died when they were little. When I was in my teens, we were three boys and three girls. My father never was divorced. I never was adopted although my mother died when I was just learning to go out alone in a kayak hunting, when I was maybe fourteen or fifteen years old [or older]. My father married again.

9. I thought of something at that big Messenger Feast at Cape Mendenhall. I saw wonderful things there. There were two shamans performing. One had a large carved wooden head of a man with much smaller carved wooden body (with arms and legs). That shaman used this to call his spirits or to show the power of his spirits. Sometimes people could hear the voices of the spirits but not that time. The other shaman had a woven fish trap. The two shamans, together, took the big wooden mask and the fish trap out of the kazigi and carried them around it. That's all—I

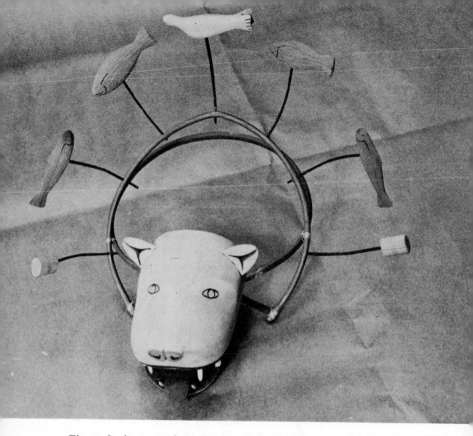

Figure 3. An unusual mask representing a dog, carved by Luther, which is not intended to cover the face but to project from the forehead.

can't remember anything else that they did. Then the men put on all kinds of wooden masks and had many dances. Aaron Lukhtusi´Gakh was the big man at Cape Mendenhall at that time—a wealthy man.

10. Another time, after my family moved to Naga´Gamiut, my two older brothers went to Nash Harbor to invite people to the Men and Women's Exchange Feast, not all the people, but they invited Dan Johnson's foster grandfather, Awi´giyakh, and his family. When the men gave the women presents and the women gave presents to the men, they did not have the right to sleep together. They did not do that, the way they did on the mainland. When my brothers went to invite people they said a dog would be hung up—that was the way of inviting. They didn't actually hang up a dog or kill one.

11. Iga´lokh was my older brother, a wealthy man, a strong man. Iga´lokh and my other brothers helped me a lot. Daniel's wife, Amelia, is my older sister. She was married to another man before Daniel. She is the only one in my family now.

12. People used to separate very easily and often. Many chil-

dren were adopted. Things were no different [in regard to family life?] when I was a boy from the way they are now. Not so many people died, though. They didn't have TB. So many women have TB now. There was an epidemic: people had bad colds and died [influenza epidemic]. Many died, as in the measles epidemic in 1942.

COMMENTS

This autobiography, incomplete as it is, still tells enough to suggest why Luther married his stepmother. Being the babied youngest child in a large and well-to-do family, he evidently remained an immature, dependent person who could not leave the protection of the family. Luther's stepmother had adopted Ernest Norton's siblings when she was married to Anigi'lakh, before she married Luther's father. Then she and U´mian, Luther's father, adopted Ernest, which explains the shared surname of these men. Although she did not have children of her own, these adoptions probably made the stepmother an ever stronger mother figure.

If the village records are correct, Luther when only eighteen or twenty years old had married a woman thirty years (or more) older than he.

What the masks and dances meant to Luther cannot be stated definitely. They may have symbolized happy times in his childhood and early manhood.

His paternal grandfather was Aiya´qsaq, the wealthy man mentioned by Daniel; and his father was not a poor hunter. The currently poor appearance of his family was not due to initial poverty and poor training, but probably to his wife's bad health and slow, heavy movement, the absence of a son or older daughter to help them, and Luther's lack of strong drive and good organization. Having always been helped, he still needed help but could not get it.

RALPH JOHNSON

Ralph was thirty-three years old, married to a woman about forty-eight years old, an unusually vigorous and healthy woman who had borne eight children before she married him. Ralph and this present wife, Rose (for a long time wife of Isaac Aiya´qsaq, mentioned in Oliver's autobiography), had one child, a two-year-old girl who was bright, pretty, and charming. Ralph rarely was seen without his little girl, Harriet, usually riding piggyback. He was clean, quite well dressed in store clothes, had considerable familiarity with white men's ways, and spoke English brokenly. But he was a homely man, occasionally apprehensive and indecisive, obviously unsure of himself and in need of direction. At times he appeared to have not quite average intelligence, at other times he seemed to be quite intelligent. His real difficulty was his unhappiness. Ralph gave the following information in the course of several conversations.

When Ralph was a boy, children threw long feathered darts across the snow, played tag, and slid down hills in winter. They could do that especially at Nash Harbor, where he grew up, because of the high hill behind the village. They did not have many games, though.

His mother died when he was about fourteen. He did not mention his father, who had died earlier. Although Ralph was considered an illegitimate child, old people would give the name of his putative father. Actually, he may have had a white father, never mentioned. He had several Caucasian physical traits.

His maternal uncle Benson adopted him. Ralph's first kayak of his own was built by Benson. He thought Benson could carve anything. (The uncle made the most beautiful wooden dishes but was not so good an ivory carver as a few other men.) Benson was a very good kayak maker. Ralph thought he was fifteen years old when he started to hunt in a kayak.

He liked Nash Harbor where he grew up. If his first wife and girls had not died, he probably still would be in Nash Harbor, but perhaps it was better that he moved to Mekoryuk (in order to marry Rose). He could get work at the Reindeer Project. He talked along this line as if arguing with himself.

When he was a boy, Anigi'lakh was a very rich man, boss of the big kazigi at Nash Harbor. "I used to look at him, and wonder." Ralph's manner expressed wonderment and admiration, but he did not suggest, as some others did, that he himself was striving for such wealth.

In the same period, James Chani'ko'guyakh was boss of the small kazigi where Ralph stayed because his uncle did. That was twenty to twenty-five years before 1946. (See Christine Gregory's Autobiography, pp. 33-34.)

Ralph said nothing about his older half brother, Dan, who also lived at Nash Harbor. Dan, however, had been adopted by James Chani'ko'guyakh and he was six years older than Ralph, so that the boys were not closely associated.

Ralph was asked whether he ever had known a period of hunger at Nash Harbor, where he had lived all his life except one year—when he was seventeen years old—and the past three years. He had known a few such times, one time especially. The men got very few seals, so they had little seal oil. It was used up long before winter was ended. They had some dried fish, but even though they possessed dried fish, they could not eat. People got thin and weak because they had no oil.

When Ralph was in his middle twenties, about the time he married Martha, Benson and his family had moved to Mekoryuk. Benson's family then included his adopted daughters, Marian and Sophie (from different families) and Marian's young son, Louis. Ralph remained at Nash Harbor with Martha's foster father, Harmon, and his family.

Without mentioning that Martha, when a young girl, had borne a son by a half-Eskimo teacher stationed at Nash Harbor, Ralph talked about the various teachers whom they had had. The teacher who had taken Martha came in 1928 and stayed six years. (Others said seven.) He was a good man when he first came. He was the first one who really preached Christianity on the island; then he took to drinking and went after women. He did not help the cause of Christianity any. After he left Nunivak, he really "went bad," Ralph said.

Martha married another man in 1933, then after his death married Ralph in the winter of 1935-36. (No one ever mentioned that

first marriage. I learned about it from records.) When Ralph and
Martha married, they were young and in love. Martha's illegitimate son, Arnold, had been adopted by her foster father Harmon,
but he was accepted by Ralph and they all lived in the same household. Ralph and Martha had two girls, born in 1939 and 1941.

Ralph then told what happened to his family in the measles epidemic in 1942. They were staying at a fish camp two or three miles
east of Nash Harbor in late summertime. The only people there
were Martha, himself, the two little girls, Richard Chappel Ka´N-
alikh and his wife, Jessie. One of Ralph's girls died, the older
one and his favorite one. The whole family was ill. The next day
the younger girl died, and two days later, Ralph's wife died. Richard did not have the measles, but he was a cripple, unable to walk
or stand without crutches, hence could not dig a grave and carry
the bodies to it. Jessie was not strong and could not do that. Although Ralph himself was ill, he got up and walked to Nash Harbor.
He was very weak and it was hard for him. Ernest Norton and
Lewis went out to the camp "to bury my family." Ralph's limited
English could not express how he had felt, but he indicated that
the loss of his whole family in four days, except his stepson, had
been a very great shock.

At this time (fall, 1946) he said he was having trouble and wanted
information and advice from me and from the teacher. The council
had turned down a request he had made and he was trying, in reality, to appeal from the council's decision. He sought us out separately; we both listened to his story, but both refrained from enter-
ing the controversy. The difficulty was that Ralph wanted Arnold.
He said Arnold was the first child he had cared for when he married Martha. He loved Arnold and every time he saw him was reminded of that early period in his marriage. He wanted Arnold
to live with him. When Martha and the two girls died (and Ralph
lost his ties with Martha's family), Arnold was taken by Harmon
and was still living with him.

I asked what his present wife, Rose, wanted. She wanted Arnold,
too. (He did not speak so strongly for Rose as for himself, however.) I asked how Arnold felt about it all. Ralph did not know,
except that one day late that summer Arnold had told Rose that he
did not want to return to Nash Harbor for the winter. (This may
have been chiefly a reluctance to live in the small dull village of
Nash Harbor, expressed by other children, rather than a reluctance
to live with Harmon.) Ralph thought that Arnold was not happy with
Harmon and Elizabeth because there was trouble in that family,
and a child was affected by trouble among older people. He referred

to Elizabeth as his sister, actually his half sister, in a noncommittal way.

Although I had not heard from other sources that Harmon and
Elizabeth were unhappy together, Ralph may have been right. Each
had lost the spouse of many years' marital life—Harmon losing
his wife only the preceding year—and they probably were having
difficulty making a new marital adjustment.

Ralph said he would take care of Arnold to the best of his ability.
He repeated that whenever he saw Arnold, he wanted him. Apparently unable to deal successfully with Harmon directly or afraid
to confront him, Ralph had appealed to the council for help. Tim,
his nephew Jeffrey, and Ernest were in favor of his having Arnold.
Ralph said that Ernest knew, from long residence at Nash Harbor,
how much Ralph cared for Arnold. Lewis, Duncan, and Paul were
against his having Arnold. He guessed it was because they did not
like Rose. He was circumspect in expressing this idea, but he
finally made it quite clear. He did not suggest that the latter three
might have been influenced by their relationship to Harmon: Lewis
was his brother-in-law, Duncan one of his adopted sons, and Paul
a relative of both Lewis and Martha. Ralph either expressed here
his own hostility to Rose by projecting it onto the council members
or else he had accepted the cultural assumption that the council's
decisions were uninfluenced by family relationships. In reality,
the council did seem to be generally fair and objective.

The council had appealed to Mani´Ganakh for a decision because he was Martha's brother as well as a council member, the
only close relative of Arnold still living. (At this time, he had
an advanced case of pulmonary tuberculosis and died within a few
months.) Mani´Ganakh's decision was fairly satisfactory to Ralph.
Mani´Ganakh said Harmon was unhappy because his wife had died,
then his adopted son Ted had drowned. Harmon felt very bad about
Ted; so he should keep Arnold for a while to take Ted's place. But
Arnold would not forget Ralph who had taken good care of him.
If Harmon died or if Arnold, when a little older, decided that he
wanted to live with Ralph, he could do so. Mani´Ganakh was sure
that Arnold would not forget Ralph. (He probably was trying to
make the decision acceptable to Ralph.)

Ralph still was not entirely satisfied. Several times he said that
he would like to get clothing for Arnold, but couldn't. He did not
explain this statement.

Ralph brought up another aspect of the controversy that the council had not mentioned. He pointed out that even though Harmon did
miss Ted and want a boy, he did not need Arnold. "He has lots of

boys. " This was true since he had Elizabeth's three sons, his adopted son Alfred (in the Navy at that moment, however), and an adopted daughter's husband, Joel. Ralph did not state that he had no son to help him although of course he and I were both quite aware of that fact. Ralph had to support Louise, Rose's child by a previous marriage, as well as his own little girl. Rose's sons were married and had to support their own growing families or were away at boarding school or otherwise unable to help their mother and stepfather.

Ralph was not a strong personality and not a good hunter, while Rose was a forceful person; as a result, she dominated him. I observed that more than once she went fishing with her daughter and son-in-law, leaving Ralph at home to care for the two little girls. Ralph was quite a good reindeer herder and undoubtedly could have been a somewhat more effective person if he had been happily married and had been given encouragement and suggestion rather than outright bossing.

Because he did not excel in terms of the old culture (hunting, ivory carving, etc.), he sought recognition in white men's ways. He pointed out with pride that Harriet, not yet three years old, was learning English, which was unusual among Nunivak children of her age. Ralph was making a special effort to teach it to her. He said it was too bad that Rose did not know much English. (He needed to state his own superiority in something.) He not only wore store clothes most of the time—I saw him hanging up freshly laundered bedsheets one day, the only time during this visit that I saw sheets in Mekoryuk.

Ralph talked almost constantly to Harriet, who was especially appealing to him just then because she was the same age as his eldest daughter was when she died, and Harriet resembled that elder half sister. He paid no attention to his stepdaughter, Louise, then seven years old. On these occasions when Ralph talked to or about Harriet, Louise looked hurt, with the look of the rejected child. Her projective tests showed that she was genuinely disturbed, symbolizing her difficulties in unusual ways. The basic difficulty seemed to relate to her mother's marriage to Ralph. Therefore I paid special favorable attention to her whenever she was present during these conversations with Ralph, and finally mentioned Louise to him twice when he talked about Arnold, saying that since Harmon would not give up Arnold, Ralph could be a father to Louise and could help her instead. She had lost her own father, just as Ralph had lost his two daughters, in the measles epidemic. Ralph behaved as if he had not heard me at all. He continued talking about his unhappiness regarding the Arnold argument. This was to be expected, since Louise could not have the same symbolic value for him as Arnold had; and Ralph was not sufficiently sure of himself to get outside his own troubles and look at Louise objectively, disregarding his own needs. Unfortunately, Louise was not an especially attractive child, in either personality or appearance. She clung to her mother and did get some affection from her while Ralph was feeling his way through his own problem.

FOUR YOUNG HUNTERS

OLIVER

Dick Lewis, Interpreter

Oliver and Ethan were half brothers, having had the same mother, and they looked very much alike. Both had unusually high coloring, obviously an inherited trait, as their mother's brother and one of his sons and most of their own children showed the same round, red-cheeked physiognomy. It gave them a healthier appearance than that of most Nunivakers, Oliver especially being a sturdy-looking, deep-chested, energetic man. He and Ethan and Ethan's young daughter June all showed at times quick forceful movements, giving the impression that they were jabbing or throwing themselves at their environment. They were not always well co-ordinated. Their behavior can be summed up as being a bit excitable. Although I never saw their mother, I would surmise that she also was a vigorous person, since she had outlived five husbands.

From infancy, Oliver and Ethan had been reared separately: Ethan, elder of the brothers, remained with his mother at least part of the time while Oliver was continuously separated from her. Ethan had not become a really successful hunter although he managed to feed his family, but Oliver was gaining noticeable success. One day, having heard that he had been "top man" at Nash Harbor the preceding spring, that is, had caught more oogruk than any other hunter, I said on encountering him at the entrance to the store, "I hear that you are getting to be noga 'Lpiakh [best hunter; wealthy man] at Nash Harbor." Oliver was delighted and told everyone who came out of the store that I had called him noga 'Lpiakh. Ethan's greater emotionality, restlessness, and tenseness adequately explain his difficulties in hunting. Also, he did not have the advantages of family assistance that Oliver had had in recent years. The latter was about thirty-two or thirty-three years old and Ethan about thirty-six when they gave these autobiographical sketches.

Oliver perhaps talked about his need and drive to be a good hunter, to the exclusion of his other drives, because we had talked about it previously. Yet there can be little doubt that this was his great interest in life.

1. First thing I remember, I was riding in a sled, but I don't remember where I was going or whom I was with.

2. Next thing I remember, I was living with an old couple. I thought they were my parents, but they really were my grandparents, I learned later. After a while, some children told me they were my grandparents. At first, I wouldn't believe them, but gradually I believed them.

3. I got my first little bird with a bow and arrow when I was living with my grandfather. My grandfather hung it in the kazigi for me. He gave food to the people, and an old man prayed for success for me, and we did the other things that people do in honor of the first little bird.

4. My grandfather made me wear an i´noGo in a little sack tied around my neck. He told me to put it in my mouth when I needed its help. I never knew what it was; I never tried to get it out of the sack.

5. Then my grandfather died. That was the first time I had seen a dead person.

6. I went to live with my father's sister named ANa´Gakh. She was poor and I had a very bad time while I was with her. I did not like it that I was poor. When other people put on new clothes for the ceremonies, I wanted new clothes, but I didn't have any. I had plenty of lice then too.

7. I don't know how long I lived with my grandparents or with my aunt. Then Isaac Aiya´qsaq took me: he was my father's brother. Isaac was married to Rose then. I was about the size of Lars [i. e., eight or nine years old] when I went to live with Isaac. My aunt lived at I´ta´gamiut; Isaac and his family didn't live at any one place; they traveled around from village to village. Isaac was good to me, and things were much better after I went to live with him, although I still was poor.

8. When I went to Isaac, I learned for the first time that I had a real mother and real brother somewhere.

9. In the Bladder Feast, I was scared when the spirits came in. I was living with Isaac when I saw the first Bladder Feast that I can remember clearly now. The spirit had grass and a mitten tied

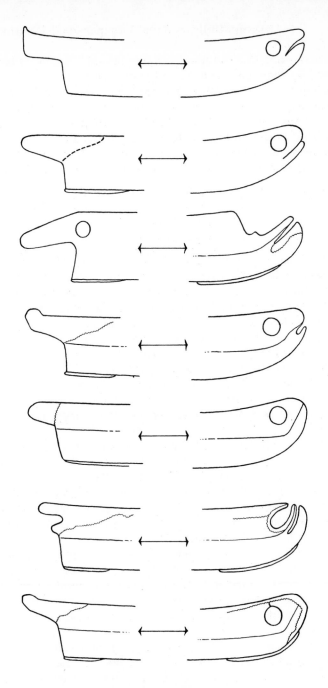

Figure 4. Examples of personal variations of bow and stern design, drawn from kayaks in use at Mekoryuk and Nash Harbor, 1939-40.

on his forehead. The old men said they would hide me. I believed them and let them put me down in the entrance. The spirit started to take me out, but I resisted and the spirit let me go. The spirit went out and the women in the entranceway cried as if they were scared. I was wearing a raven-head cap. I remember the two old men sitting in the middle of the kazigi, talking about the eiders, and the man and two boys acting like eiders. One man took a dog's head and threw it down on the floor. The old men sang:

> ma´mmakukaNa´si--se-e-e
> maLi´khse-e-e
> a´Na´lukaNa´si--e-e
> taku´kaGamakhsala´si

10. The man who was chosen to jump around the old men, with sticks, was called ni´nakamakh. The old men sang for him, a song starting "ni´nakamakh." I can't remember the rest of it.

11. Each man imitated and then named his real i´noGo. Mine was raven. Besides the raven cap, I had a belt made of a raven beak wrapped in sealskin. My ki´Lka is dog. ki´Lka is different from i´noGo. Before they put the bladders down under the ice, the men talked to the seals, telling them to return.

12. I had my own little drum, with a puffin handle, at this time.

13. The next night after the end of the Bladder Feast, the women came in and danced. The men played with the women, teased them, had fun.

14. Then Aaron Lukhtusi´Gakh, who was the wealthy man on the south side then, gave painted sticks, with dog hair on the end of the sticks, to the messengers to carry to other villages. After the messengers left, the men made the animals for the trays.

15. My family went out to seal camp in the spring. When they were working on the kayaks [i.e., repairing them, putting on fresh cover, etc.], they did not eat.

16. When a man came in bringing oogruk, I ran with the other boys to that man. I had a little hook for blubber and when the man gave me blubber, I put it on the hook and ran home. I remember being poor. I wanted to get seals, so to catch seals [and be rich] I would go out at night and sweep the kazigi entranceway. People told me to do that.

17. Isaac made me a kayak, shaped like a knife. It was straight, had no hole in the bow. It had a tray to hold the harpoon line and two paddles and an ice hook [etc.]. I killed a spotted seal the year I got my first kayak.

18. When I came back to the village after I got the seal, the men

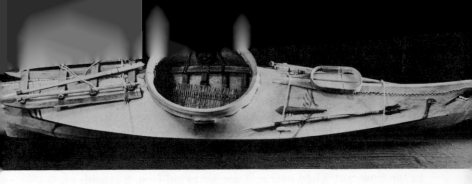

Figure 5. Child's large model kayak, showing painted bird design on cover, design of bow and stern, carved face of protective spirit on cockpit support, painted design on harpoon-line holder, carved ivory pieces on retaining thong across deck, design on paddle, all of which individualize each kayak. These help to explain Oliver's identification with his kayak.

wouldn't let me eat. That night Mike told me to wash, and he stuck a needle in the end of each of my fingers, just a little. He told me to put on mittens. That night they let me eat. At the next Bladder Feast they would not let me eat for three days. I had a headache and I felt bad. When they let me eat, I could eat only a little at first: I had no appetite.

19. Different families did different things when a boy got his first seal. Some told the boy to stay awake. Some took off all his clothes. And so on.

20. My next kayak had a hole in the bow. It was made by Isaac, too. It had everything to go with it: kayak mat, meat hook, ice hook [etc.]. I caught walrus and every kind of seal with it.

21. I tried to help Isaac; I wanted to help him. But then Isaac died, the year the church was built [in 1936, when Oliver was twenty-two or twenty-three years old]. A year later, or a little more than a year later, I married Agnes, Lewis' daughter, Dick's sister, and I came to live with Lewis at Nash Harbor. Lewis' home was a good place. Lewis was like a father to me.

22. From then on, I did well. I killed more oogruk and trapped more fox. Now I never sleep when the weather is good in seal-hunting season. I am always out hunting.

23. Once I fell, slipped down on some rocks and hurt my back and side. A bone in my side is crooked now. So now I don't go so far out in hunting seals. But when I go trapping, I go much farther with skis now than I used to go when just walking. Years ago, when we tied dogs at the side of the sled, they got tired and I had to push the sled. I would get hot and tired. Now when I get tired or cold, I sit in the sled and wrap up. I don't walk much if I have a good leader. Sometimes, with poor dogs, it's hard work, though.

24. I have had four children. My little girl died of measles in 1942. I have three boys now.

25. I want to get rich, but I'm not rich yet.

26. I thought of something that happened when I was first married, or maybe I had been married a year or two. Dick and I went out to get wood one day. We were playing, trying to throw the wood as far as we could, and such things. Dick threw a big piece—it hit my kayak and broke it right in two. It was that kayak with a hole in the bow that I had before I got married [much laughter].

NOTES

2. Although his words suggest shock in learning that he did not have parents, his tone and facial expression were matter-of-fact, with no present evidence of shock. He said in effect that he had thought the children were fooling him, teasing him and trying to scare him, and he simply didn't believe them. Apparently it was weeks or months before other evidence accumulated and he accepted it.

4. This statement was made in answer to a question. This and other items show that Oliver was more submissive than several others of his age, (e.g., Christine). He wanted very much to be attached to a father figure, to belong to a family, and he was submissive to such a person.

6. Apparently it was Oliver's paternal grandfather, who had been a successful hunter and well-to-do man, who adopted him. The poor aunt who next adopted Oliver was Gregory's mother.

7. Isaac was not actually Oliver's father's brother, but had married his father's parallel cousin (i.e., "sister").

The statement regarding length of time was made in answer to my question. He must have been quite young when living with his grandparents, yet old enough to use bow and arrow, perhaps five or six years old. The slow and emphatic way in which he told of his difficult period with his aunt conveyed to me a strong impression that he had remained with her several years, when about seven or eight years old. His experience had been a continuing frustration rather than a momentary discomfiture.

Isaac had several small children of his own at that time, and it must have been difficult for him to provide for all of them.

9. Oliver said later, in answer to my question, that he learned the true identity of the Bladder Feast spirits from other people. He didn't find out by himself, showing again his submission to his elders. He did not seek to remain a child, however. He had a strong drive to grow up, at least in overt behavior, and to be identified with his elders. He wanted to act and believe as he thought they acted and believed.

He was not sure what the song meant. I had not heard this Bladder Feast song previously.

11. Since others had said there was no essential difference between an i´noGo and a ki´Lka, I asked about this point. Oliver was certain that they were different, demonstrated by the fact that his were two different animals. It might still have been true that in principle they were not different, but I did not discuss them fur-

ther in order not to distract him from his account. His interest in the iˊnoGos shows his interest in belonging to the family and having its iˊnoGos. They symbolize the family; they are its totems.

12. This refers to the wooden handle carved like a puffin head. It shows that the drum was not decorated like the totem. I asked him whether he had his own drum at that age, to get some idea as to how actively children participated in the ceremony. Drumming did not seem to mean much to the children.

13. This was sexual play, ordinarily ending in the Men and Women's Exchange. Oliver probably was becoming more interested in heterosexual relations at that time.

14. These trays were large compositions of small wooden figures representing hunting deeds of the ancestors. Oliver's mentioning them is significant. Compare his account with others' accounts of Messenger Feasts.

16. Compare with Richard Chappel's statement.

17. Oliver named each piece of gear for the kayak, in a tone indicating that this was important to him. I did not record all the items.

19. This was given in answer to my question as to whether all boys had to do the same things when they caught their first seal.

20. Again he named all the gear proudly, listing even more items this time.

21. Oliver may have said this with special emphasis because Dick Lewis was present. Yet Oliver and Lewis did seem to get along well. Lewis, as chief of Nash Harbor even before he became chief of the whole island, was bound to help a young man like Oliver. That was his duty, and he was glad to have a young man to help him before Dick was old enough to hunt.

22. Oliver seemed to be expressing a compulsion to hunt.

23. This type of accident, breaking a rib, cracking a vertebra, was not unusual.

26. Although seemingly both were laughing good-naturedly—at their boyish antics and their consternation on breaking the kayak— there was a little accusation on Oliver's part and a little embarrassment on Dick's part. A kayak is a valuable possession and this one was especially valuable to Oliver. He and his wife, Agnes, seemed to be quite congenial with Dick, Agnes's younger brother. When all of them were in Mekoryuk, Dick often ate with Agnes and Oliver rather than with other relatives.

ETHAN

Charlie Sharp, Interpreter

Ethan, who was about the same age as Christine, thus older than Dick Lewis and Frederick Matthew, was asked to tell about his life as a hunter: everything he could remember that was connected with hunting. He was not an outstandingly good hunter, but he had shown an interest in fishing camps, the types of fish that are found around Nunivak and in other items of natural history.

1. As a boy, I tried to catch mink. I had one small trap, fastened with stick and string. I caught mink and sold them. I caught them in the summer because Ermeloff [trader] wanted summer mink.

2. In the fall, I got one white fox. I was proud of it—I covered it with my rain parka to keep it from getting bloody. I was about the size of Jim Dennis then [twelve or thirteen years old]. I lived at Cape Mendenhall.

3. The next summer I found a little walrus sleeping on the rocks. I shot it and called the village. We were living at Nago´yatali´-gamiut then. My family used the walrus. There weren't many people at the camp, so we didn't divide it up.

4. That same summer I found a young fur seal on the beach and killed it.

5. The next winter I saw a red fox near the village and went after it, by myself. I saw tracks of polar bear that had come from the ice out onto the land; I got scared and went home. There. were two adult bears and a young one. I loaded my rifle and went home. I had my own gun at that time.

6. At the same time when I was learning to hunt, I was also seeing spirits. Should I tell about them, too? [Yes.]

7. Once, when I went out in moonlight, I saw a person with the behind of a dog. At Nugavalugamiut, another time, someone hit me on the foot with a rock. I was hurt and I cried, but I couldn't see anyone.

8. This was the first spirit that I saw: once, early in the morning, when I went out of the kazigi, I saw a stranger in the village. I followed him—I could see his tracks in the snow. The man went down to the beach, and disappeared. I couldn't find any more tracks.

9. Another time, near the kazigi someone took hold of me. I was taking my dish home after eating [in the kazigi] in the evening. I threw the dish at the man as he ran away. I went in the house and forgot the spirit. Later I got sick and vomited. From then on, I was sick. Whenever I ate, I vomited. Then I remembered the spirit and told my parents, and then I got well. I think that spirit made me forget—that's why I immediately forgot about seeing him.

10. Another time I heard something whistle. It was at I´ta´gamiut, when I was hunting, that I heard it. I often heard spirits trying to come into the house. People say that spirits pound before coming in. Before coming in, one time a spirit pounded slowly and heavily four times. In those days, people always left a house when they heard something like this outside the house. If they didn't go out, the spirit might come in and eat the people. In the evening, when I was with Fritz Russell I heard this pounding, at Cha´qawa´gamiut. I told Fritz to go out and see, but Fritz had no boots, so I went out. I didn't see anything. [See Dick Lewis's reference to Fritz Russell, who may have been mentally below normal.]

11. At that village there was a different kind of spirit: kaya´-gayakh. It looked like a kayak bow, one with a hole. People tell that once two men went to that village. (It was just a camp; people didn't live there all the time.) They heard something. They went out of the house and saw this kayak bow come out of the water. They went into another house. The kaya´gayakh went into the house they had been in, and they saw flames come from the skylight and entranceway. They slipped out and left the village very fast. This happened some time before Fritz and I were there.

12. Then Fritz and I left for home, driving reindeer. We got two red foxes along the way. We also caught a fox without a tail. It got stormy, so we went home to Nash Harbor.

13. Cho´kochokhoyagamiut [where?] was going to have a dance festival. I and Oliver came to Mekoryuk to get people. In payment, Isaac Aiya´qsaq gave me a kayak. That spring I caught a seal. I chopped wood and put sticks on the seal. All spring I got only one

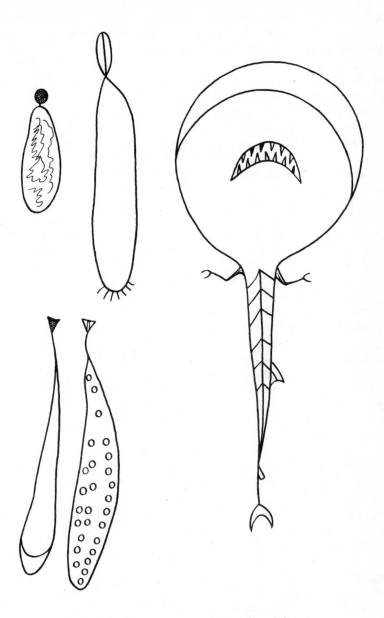

Figure 6. While talking about hunting and fishing, Ethan sketched these sea animals that he had seen. The one with large head and vicious-appearing teeth, which he called a devil-fish, evidently is intended to portray a bottom-feeding fish that can inflate the fore part of its body.

seal, a little gray seal. Rules in those days: a boy couldn't eat anything until night. He couldn't eat anything fresh until the next Bladder Feast. For five days I ate nothing at all, in the next Bladder Feast. I just drank water, and I vomited. I wasn't allowed to eat cranberries but could eat crowberries. I wore sealskin mittens and a cap all the time, even in summer.

14. When I came home after catching that seal, I washed and got ready to eat. Before I could eat, I had to suck the ends of my fingers and suck my palm, to remove dirt. I couldn't eat hot or even warm food, either. I thought that if I ate hot food, my teeth would fall out. I couldn't walk in cold water—I couldn't get wet at all. My parents gave the seal to the old people. But my mother didn't take off her earrings. (I was living with my own mother and my stepfather, who was Gregory's father.)

15. I used to wear a cap made of fish skin. I also had a cap made of a crane. I wore it in the Bladder Feast and when I went hunting for the first time in the spring. The crane was my i´noGo. I also had a white fox cap. White fox was my i´noGo, too. I had a belt of duck skin (a duck something like an eider), covered with rosin. A cormorant tail was hung around my neck. All of these were i´noGos. I had a dog fur wrist band. I put dog whiskers in the seam of the kayak cover at the stern of my kayak. There were sea gull feathers tied on the stern, tied with sealskin. I had sea lion for my i´noGo, too, and I made the huff-huff sound of sea lion before I went out of the kazigi in the Bladder Feast. I also had a puffin i´noGo. Should I tell everything like that? [I replied that these things were very important for hunting and that I would like to hear about them.]

16. My father told me after I caught oogruk to make a sound like a puffin. I think it was two years after I got my first little seal before I got a mukluk [oogruk]. When I came home after getting the mukluk, I took a piece of walrus tooth and rubbed it around my mouth. For mukluk, I did the same things as for my first little seal. I couldn't eat any mukluk oil, in addition.

17. Several people had been out hunting mukluk at the same time, so we cut my bearded seal in two. We kept one half and cut the other half in pieces and gave them to those people. We gave all of my half to ANa´sakh, who was Ezra's father, an old man. (ANa´-sakh had separated from Ezra's mother when Ezra was a small baby and had married someone else.)

18. I used to get birds and eggs from the cliffs on the west side of Nunivak, near Herbert's place. I climbed up and down the cliffs holding on to a walrus hide rope; I was scared when the waves

came right up against the cliffs. We got lots of ducks and puffins. There were eight different kinds of birds there.

19. After I had caught a bearded seal, my mother told me I should get married and picked out a wife for me. But I didn't like her and wouldn't marry her. I married the wife I have now, but I left her before long. Then I married Naya´Ganiq, daughter of Russell. I left her and married Juliet [a relative of his first wife]. We separated and I went back to my first wife, Pani´khkakh.

20. After I was married, the first time, we moved to Talu´-gamiut. We saw a walrus sleeping on the rocks. I and Herbert (my wife's brother) both shot at it. I hit it, my first adult walrus. Mani´Ganakh's wife, Juliet (she wasn't married to Mani´Ganakh then), was the first one to see it. The next morning the herders, Paul and Homer, came to Talu´gamiut. That evening Homer got a baby spotted seal there. Next day the herders left. Herbert and I divided the walrus. We did not have to give any to Juliet because she was "sister" to Herbert and got part of his share. Next day I went with Herbert to the cliffs to get ducks, but we got only a few.

21. Next fall I and my wife went to Chu´gohagamiut to get fish. We got a lot of trout. Then we moved to Nash Harbor. I went seal hunting in the fall and caught seals. That winter I got about ten white fox. I got the same price for them then as I get now, about ten dollars for the best. In the spring I moved to Cape Mendenhall, with my kayak and wife, to hunt seal. The second or third time I went out, I got oogruk. Then I caught other seals. That spring Bernard and I got a walrus together. Gregory and I went after a walrus asleep on the ice. We shot five or six times but couldn't hit it. Another time when a walrus was sleeping on the ice, Bernard and I tried to get it but it jumped into the water. We saw lots of walrus floating on a small ice block, and we went out from the village. There were also walrus in the sea. We were scared but we went after them. I pulled my kayak out on the ice where the walrus were and killed two. Then the walrus on the ice got away. The men shot and shot, but the walrus were wary—it was hard to hit them. There were lots of walrus. We poured seal oil in the water to make them go away, but the walrus stayed. We burned primus stoves and burned grass. [They feared that the walrus would tip over the kayaks.] The wind came up, so I took the skins and some meat and went home. Some other men got walrus after this: shot them from shore as they swam past. (Bernard is my partner and Gregory is my stepbrother.)

22. Then I went fishing for cod. I didn't get any—just got devil-fish [sculpin].

23. We moved to Kwiga´gamiut. There were lots of fish there: red salmon. That same summer, I went hunting for sea lion and got one.

24. In September, in silver salmon time, I went to Talu´gamiut to get birds on the cliffs. I found two dead walrus on my way to Talu´-gamiut. They had their tusks, too. I didn't get many birds, though.

25. I found a levtak [one year old oogruk] on shore. I had a dog with me, so I put the skin on the dog's back and the dog packed it home.

26. Bernard found a large dead whale. He told INakhta´gamiut to help him cut up the whale. Everybody cut pieces from the whale for themselves. At that place, I got a ring seal when I was out fishing for flounders. That was the same autumn when I found the two dead walrus. I also caught geese. There were many flounders there. We got them with a spear.

27. That winter, I caught white and red fox on the south side. And I got seals during the winter, by kayak. It was a stormy spring and hunting was not good: only a few seals and no walrus. Then late in the spring, we collected lots of eggs.

28. In the winter I returned to Talu´gamiut. Another man there got mukluk in the spring. Then I got seals, too, including mukluk.

NOTES

9. This is a case of genuine repression of the memory of a traumatic experience. (See Lantis, 1953, p. 129, regarding this phenomenon in Alaskan Eskimos.)

21. A sizable herd of walrus is not often seen near Nunivak. Although Nunivakers hunt them whenever they get a chance, nevertheless they are afraid of walrus. Ethan was here expressing a common attitude.

28. At this point another person entered, interrupting the narrative. As Ethan and the interpreter were bored with this recital and glad to quit, I did not try to continue it. Ethan appears to have been more suggestible and to have had more intense emotional reactions; therefore, it is not surprising that he had greater spiritual experience in adolescence than most Nunivakers. But was he really different, with some of the traits of a shaman, or was he simply more outspoken and confiding? It is possible that he had some basic insecurity or specific fears that he could not express directly, as Oliver, for example, revealed his need to be rich. Ethan perhaps could express his anxieties and needs only indirectly, through mystical experiences in which he projected his anxieties in supernatural form. What, for example, did the kayak-spirit mean to him?

DICK LEWIS

Dick was one of the three most acculturated young men of the island. In the period when he told the following circumstances of his life, he was night watchman at the Reindeer Project. With a steady cash income and with favors from the director of the project, he was able to wear store clothes solely and to eat store-bought food much more than others. In less obvious elements of his life, too, he was drifting away from the old Nunivak life. As he was living apart from his family, in his own little house provided by the Reindeer Project, he was rather lonely. One reason for this was because he slept during the day and so missed much activity of the village. He would come into my house at the project occasionally about eleven at night to chat. He did not always talk about himself, but in the course of four or five weeks the following information regarding his own life was given. (Not recorded in the first person.)

At this time, he was twenty-three years old, still unmarried, the only son of the chief (i. e. , president of the council).

The preceding summer, 1945, Dick had been on the mainland, trading. His home was at Nash Harbor, but he had returned first to Mekoryuk, which is closer to the mainland. By this time, he had been away from home several days. Someone came from Nash Harbor, saying that his mother was very sick. He went immediately, but she was dead when he arrived. (His eyes filled with tears when he told of this, and he had to stop a moment.) His mother had had a "bad cold," probably pneumonia. His father's sister, Harmon's wife, died a couple of days later, of the same sickness. Neither one had been sick long.

Dick felt the loss of his mother very much. During the winter, six months or so after his mother's death, his father had married Jane Matthew, widow of the former chief. Dick didn't like this.

Lewis brought Jane and her two adopted girls, Barbara and Gertrude, to their home in Nash Harbor. From then on, Dick was
somewhat estranged from his home, as he had had evidently a very
close relationship to his mother, felt her absence keenly, and could
not yet accept another woman in her place.

When we talked about his sisters, Marjory, Agnes, and Esther,
he did not show any special interest or pride in them, but he did
not show the antagonism indicated in his relationship with his stepmother and her girls. He just took his sisters for granted.

In the home constellation, Dick had had only two sisters, Esther
having been adopted by Harmon and his wife, that is, Dick's paternal aunt and her husband.

This summer, Dick did not go to Bethel to trade. His father
had put the seal oil and skins from Dick's spring sealing with his
own catch and traded them on the mainland. Dick did not know what
his father had been paid for the family's products. He received
no accounting. His father had bought things that the family needed,
including of course clothing and other things for Dick. This information was given largely in response to my questioning. Dick
showed little resentment—it was all right for his father to handle
the family's business.

Dick owned seven dogs; his father had none. His father did not
go trapping, hence seldom needed dogs. Dick owned one kayak and
a new fifteen-foot plank boat that he had built himself. He was using
sails as he did not have a motor for it yet. His father had a cabin
launch that was old but still in good condition. Dick owned six guns
of various calibers. He had owned two more but had given one to
his brother-in-law Oliver, and had sold one. At Nash Harbor he
had a little frame house that he had built himself. He did not live
with his father and stepmother.

His family was talking about staying in Mekoryuk next winter.
He wanted to return to Nash Harbor, which he liked better: it had
plenty of good running water all year—no hauling ice—and there was
good hunting on the west side of the island, over beyond Nash Harbor. (He may have been interested in some girl there.)

Lewis had been "getting after" Dick to stop smoking. (As chief,
Lewis had to enforce the village rule of no smoking, and also may
have objected personally to smoking.) Dick had quit smoking, to
please his father, although the director of the project encouraged
him to smoke.

Dick's family not long before had tried to get him to marry Claudia Field, a tall, thin girl with pulmonary tuberculosis (not known
at this time). Paul Scott, cousin of Claudia and her chief support,

also had approved. But Dick would not have her. He said she was too tall. (She was shy, not especially feminine or lively although she had a rather pretty face, was a good worker, and came from a good family.) Otherwise, Dick was noncommittal regarding specific girls. One time I said that Clarissa, Ted Cook's widow, was good-looking. Dick said, "That's what they say. " He looked at me quizzically over the top of his glasses. Clarissa, however, was well advanced in pregnancy and not likely to marry until after the child was born.

Another time I showed him designs made by Emily Norton and praised them for their color composition. Dick showed interest and pleasure in them, but he would not talk about Emily herself. He did make it plain that he did not want Kate, another young widow, either. He said, "There are no girls on Nunivak. " He was going to the mainland to get married. (But the next spring he married a very shy, immature Nunivak girl who had never been married previously.) He said he dreamed about women, but would not tell about which ones he dreamed.

"People came after Agnes, " his sister, trying to arrange a marriage when she was only about fifteen years old. His father said she was too young, she should wait. She was not married until she was eighteen or nineteen years old.

Dick did not dream much, and when he did, he could not remember the dreams in the morning. Once he had had a nightmare: he fell off a cliff near Nash Harbor down onto the rocks. He woke up, surprised to find that he was not hurt. He said, "Even though I fall down, I'm not hurt. " (Apparently he still believed that one really travels in dreams.)

When he was about twelve years old and habitually sleeping in the kazigi, sometimes he walked in his sleep. One time, when he awoke, he was lying outside the kazigi entrance. He had gone out there to sleep. But he had not walked in his sleep in recent years.

The cause of the loss-of-support type of nightmare, the falling down a cliff, could not be ascertained by superficial questioning. I did not try to probe deeply at that time.

When Dick was a boy, he had heard the old people tell a story about an old woman who had lived on the east side of the island.

She sent her two young daughters—perhaps they were granddaughters—out to get water. They came back saying that they had heard something out among the ice, coming toward shore. The old woman was a shaman. She took her shaman-doll ("It was a wooden figure nearly as big as a man") and the girls down to the edge of the ice. They set the doll up in front of them to protect them. They saw a man coming to shore in a kayak frame, with no cover. He got out of the kayak, went up to their house, and went in. While he was inside, they saw fire coming out of the skylight. When he didn't find them, he came out, came down past them, got in his kayak, and went away. "Those people are all dead now, but this really happened." Whenever the old men in the kazigi told stories like this, when Dick was a boy, he was very frightened and would not go outdoors at night.

One night, only a few years before, Dick was sleeping in the kazigi next to Paul Scott, his father's cousin. He woke up and saw something like a man standing beside him, except that that spirit had a light shining inside him. It looked white all over and glowing (like a light shining behind a sheet). The spirit took hold of his wrist and Dick, very frightened, kicked Paul to waken him. Paul didn't wake up, but the spirit let go of Dick's wrist and "sort of disappeared." Then Dick saw it again and succeeded in waking Paul this time. The spirit went out the underground entrance, but just as it was going out, Paul got up and saw it and went out after it. When he got outside, he saw nothing. This experience gave Dick an extreme fright.

A few years before, on December 24, Dick had heard bells ringing in the sky, during the night. The next day when he told his family, Agnes said she had heard them, too. Dick had been sleeping in the kazigi, Agnes in the house.

Dick said he had heard tukai´yuli, "little people," pounding but never had seen any. Fritz Russell and a man, since died, once had seen one in a pond. They saw him plainly. There was no question that it was a tukai´yuli standing in the sedges.

Dick had found out the true nature of the spirits in the Bladder Feast when he was very young. Perhaps he was as young as four or five years old. Dick thought he had acted because of suspicion—"Maybe I was too wise for them!"—but more likely self-protection and resistance motivated him. Anyway, he knew about the spirits punishing children and so had concealed a sharp stick in his boot. The people gave Duncan Cook to the spirit immediately before Dick. Duncan was three or four years older than Dick and fought the spirit hard: tore his clothes. Then Dick poked him with the stick. The spirit was plainly revealed to be Gregory.

Until he was approximately twelve years old, Dick always ate with his fingers. He didn't know how to use a knife and fork until then. He had learned how from the family of Mr. Nagozruk, the schoolteacher.

Dick laughed at himself, or seemed to, but actually he spoke with pride. Many children on Nunivak still never had used a fork in eating.

When he was about fifteen years old, one time he pounded a brass shell in his gun. (He gave an elaborate technical explanation regarding the gun and shell.) The shell exploded, injuring his right hand and his face. He was blinded. It happened when he was out hunting alone, across the river from Nash Harbor. He went toward the sound of the stream, and when he reached it, people in the village saw him and brought him across to the teacher. Mr. Nagozruk washed his eyes many times to remove the powder. Then with fine tweezers he picked bits of shell from Dick's face and treated him for powder burns. After his eyes had been washed, he could see light, but that was all. He stayed in the house three or four days, and his sight gradually returned. "Now I'm O. K. —no scars or anything."

His parents had told him that Arnold Ermeloff was his serious partner because his father and Arnold's mother, Martha, had been partners. But his parents never had mentioned any other partners. (Dick was rather defensive about this, knowing that most Nunivakers have many partners. He need not have been, since possibly families who had been partners of his family had died out. Alternatively, there may have been some loss in recognition of partnership obligations.) To demonstrate that he was not concealing any such information from me, Dick told me that his father's father was named A ʾlali ʾkakh. He did not know his father's mother's name or her relationship to Russell. He just knew that people had told him he was related to Russell's family. He guessed they were his cousins. His family had told him how to do right, be honest, respect obligations, etc., but they never had explained family relationships.

Russell's daughter, Mary, had said that she called Dick her older brother, so I asked him whether he had thought of Russell's children as his brothers and sisters (i. e., parallel cousins) when he was young. No, he always had thought of them as cousins. He was correct: Russell's children were cross-cousins of Dick's father.

Dick's desire to establish himself apart from his family and to live in a more modern manner, which had begun to develop before his mother's death, had been implemented by a considerate and generous white man, the superintendent of the Reindeer Project in previous years. He had helped Dick get lumber to build his own house at Nash Harbor. Dick had admired him very much and turned to him even more after his mother's death. Unfortunately, that

man had not returned to the project this summer. The new superintendent made Dick his only favorite and confidant, but Dick saw
his faults and did not respect him.

The preceding spring, for the big seal hunt by kayak, Dick had
gone to Talu´gamiut on the west side of the island. He had caught
three mukluk, one levtak (young bearded seal), five big spotted
seals, and four common hair seals or harbor seals. This was a
good catch for a young hunter.

FREDERICK MATTHEW

Like Dick Lewis, Fred was a lonely young man, nineteen years old and unmarried. He was an orphan. His stepmother, Jane, had moved to Nash Harbor to live with her brother Joel, after the sudden death of Fred's father in 1944. Then she had married Lewis, who also lived in Nash Harbor. Fred had remained in Mekoryuk with his older brother, Jeffrey. The boys' father, Matthew Larson, whom I had known in 1939 and 1940, had been "chief" of the island, a hard-working, ambitious, autocratic man. In the late spring and summer of 1940 Matthew had built a twenty-foot cabin launch. He had slept in a tent beside the hull, and sometimes when he could not sleep, thinking of all that he had to do and wanted to do, he would be heard at two in the morning hammering away at his boat.

Fred gave much of the following information, at various times and not in chronological order. The remainder was obtained from older people and from my own observation.

After hearing Nicholas tell of his childhood, Fred said regretfully that he was sorry he could not remember his boyhood. After his mother died, A´qoaq's mother, Nu´san, had taken him. His paternal grandmother, who lived with the family during much of Fred's boyhood, was already quite old when he was born. She did not take care of him. (See Edwin Larson.) He could not remember A´qoaq's mother caring for him. He had been told about that. Nu´san was related to him by marriage: her husband's brother was Fred's maternal grandfather. Knowing this but without telling Fred, I asked him about his grandfathers: their names and their relationship to Nu´san. Fred said, sincerely, I believe, that he did not know his grandfathers' names, hence did not realize that he was named for his maternal grandfather, Chani´aGa´Lagia.

Fred's father had then married Marian, who bore Owen when Fred was only three years old. Fred's mother must have died at

his birth or during his infancy, because his father had remarried
and begotten Owen before Fred was three years old. Fred could
not remember anything regarding Owen's birth, but he lived with
his father and stepmother from then on. He remembered Marian
taking care of him. His father had been married to her "a long
time." He thought he was eleven or twelve years old when they
separated, but he probably was only six or seven years old. When
Fred was that age, Marian bore an illegitimate son, said to be the
son of a part white, part Eskimo man. This boy was adopted and
reared by Marian's foster parents. It is not likely that Matthew
and Marian continued to live together after the birth of her illegitimate child. In any case, Matthew and Jane had married and she
had borne a son, who soon died, before Fred was twelve years old.
Fred's claim that he could not remember much from his childhood
seems verified. But he remembered when Marian left. When I
asked him how he felt, he said he was "not glad." Marian was the
only mother figure he could remember and it had been hard for
him when she and Matthew separated. Fred showed a favorable
interest in her even though by this time she was looked upon very
unfavorably by most of the village. For example, he was interested
in learning from my records, when he saw me copying them one
time, that Marian was then thirty-five years old. He did not seem
to be interested in others.

The three boys, Jeffrey, Fred, and Owen, had been kept by Matthew. As Jeffrey was five years older than Fred, they did not play
together. Fred played with Noah Austin, Jimmie Dennis, and sometimes Charlie Sharp and Adolph Wilson. Charlie lived over on the
east side, on Etolin Strait, but he came to Mekoryuk occasionally.
Raymond Field had not moved to Mekoryuk yet, but by the time
Fred was twelve, he had joined this age group.

Fred remembered the first little bird he shot, with bow and arrow. His family stretched and dried the skin and hung it in the
kazigi at the Bladder Feast. His father gave presents in honor of
the little bird.

Fred said he was naughty sometimes, but he did not remember
any one time especially.

When he was about thirteen years old, he found a hair seal pup
on the beach of a little island near Mekoryuk. He picked it up and
put it up on the bank, on the grass. It flopped down to the beach,
a drop of about three and a half feet. He brought it home and then
killed it. Up to now (1946) he had brought home four live seal pups,
including a spotted seal. His father's name, Nai´Gakh, meant
"young seal." Jeffrey had brought home the live seal pup that I

had seen in 1940, a picture of which had been published (Lantis, 1941).

Fred did not remember much about the Bladder Feast. None had been given at Mekoryuk since he was about eleven years old. He could not remember which men had taken the special parts in the Feast. He knew the names of various spirits, but did not know all the requirements and tabus relative to them. He had never heard about not stepping over a crack or details of the belief concerning pla´qa-pla´ga, and others about which I asked him. Fred belonged to the postmissionary generation, his entire adolescence—most important period in a Nunivak man's religious development—having occurred after the arrival of the missionary.

By the age of thirteen, Fred had been given his own kayak by his father, but it was not a new one. It was a hand-me-down, still in good condition. At that time, Jeffrey was given a new kayak, as he was starting to hunt on the ice in the big spring hunt.

Fred had gone to school only three years and had quit at fifteen. He had had no opportunity to go to school earlier, as there had been none in Mekoryuk where his family had lived for a long time. Owen had been able to start younger and continue in school longer and had been sent to White Mountain Boarding School. He was there now. Fred's attitude toward Owen was not ascertained definitely. He apparently felt overlooked, left out, not having had the advantages of either brother and being unable to compete with them. He could not compete with Owen in use of English and book knowledge or with Jeffrey in hunting, trading, and community affairs, especially since Jeffrey recently had been elected to the council as its youngest member. Jeffrey also was a regular herder while Fred was only an occasional one. One of Fred's anxieties was indicated by his persistent allegation that he did not know English and his refusal to speak it, although he knew it nearly as well as the other youths of his age. Six years previously, he had enjoyed learning English; now he rejected it.

Upon Isaac Aiya´qsaq's death, Matthew and Jane had adopted the youngest child of Isaac and Rose, Barbara, then still in infancy. Jeffrey and Fred had placed Barbara in the "little sister" role and were very indulgent to her. She could remember no other parents and still thought of Matthew and Jane as her parents and the boys as her brothers although she now knew that Rose was her mother.

Matthew's death occurred at a crucial point in Fred's career: when he was about seventeen years old, just ready to start hunting in a kayak. Jeffrey, already married and a father, received Matthew's house and plank boat. Jeffrey and Fred together got the

seven dogs, which they increased to a team of nine good dogs.
Fred continued to live with Jeffrey and his family, and the latter
took responsibility for him. Jeffrey, with four young children to
provide for and with a high family position to maintain, had a heavy
responsibility for a young man still barely twenty-five years old.
While he probably did his best, he could not help Fred as their
father could have done. His wife, Dora, daughter of the former
trader, was over-burdened with child care, unaggressive except in
speech, and apparently dependent on others for motivation and direction. Dora's parents had been, in a sense, interlopers on Nunivak Island and, after twenty years on the island, still were regarded with envy and resentment. When the store and herd that they
managed for a Nome company were purchased by the government
and became community enterprises and they themselves left the
island, Dora was the only one of the large family who remained.
She had married Jeffrey at thirteen or fourteen years of age.

The preceding winter, Fred had gone trapping with Jeffrey and
had caught or shot nineteen foxes, including six white ones. He
had shot seven in one day. In the spring, Fred went to Cape Manning with Jeffrey for seal and walrus hunting. Jeffrey got a full-
grown walrus and Fred shot a baby walrus without tusks. But it
yielded a lot of meat and oil and he was proud of it. I asked Fred
who cut up his seals, a matter that is important to a man since
the value of skins depends largely on the skill used in skinning
and preparing them. Fred replied that Dora did, and made a wry
face showing displeasure. Dora, with little training in such work,
being the trader's daughter and married too young, undoubtedly
was unskilled and perhaps was uninterested. She seemed to lack
the Nunivaker's objective interest in such matters as technique
in skinning a seal.

Fred was much cleaner and neater than most of the young unmarried men, largely due to his own efforts. He did not like to
sleep in the kazigi with the other youths because it was damp and
dirty; therefore he slept in Jeffrey's house. That arrangement was
not satisfactory, either, since he and Dora were not congenial,
the house was small and crowded with four very young children,
and Jeffrey's love-making undoubtedly disturbed him. In the old
days, when young men invariably slept in large, well-kept kazigis,
such a family situation would not have occurred.

Fred was preoccupied by sex but unable to obtain a girl for the
kind of sexual relationship that by now he would be permitted. He
was not yet in the proper socio-economic position to marry. He
had drifted into a late-adolescent gang of boys with the reputation

of being irresponsible and insolent. They were having difficulties with both the Eskimo elders and the whites.

When Jane married Lewis, she took Barbara and a recently adopted little girl with her but in a sense deserted Fred and Owen. Fred now was estranged from her. Not knowing of this development and remembering Matthew's closely bound family, on my arrival that year I gave Jane a picture of Matthew's and her entire family that I had taken in 1940. I also gave Lewis and Jane several pictures of village scenes which he, as chief, was to keep for the community and supposedly show to the community. Later, Fred told me that Barbara had temporarily stolen and had shown to him a picture of himself. Jane had not shown to any of the children the picture including their father and grandmother and other photographs in which they were much interested. Fred now was openly resentful of Jane.

Being lonely and frustrated in establishing a satisfactory family relationship, Fred asserted his friendship for me more aggressively than the other boys. He insisted on smoking when he came to my house, in defiance of the general council rule against smoking. He said I was his friend, I would let him do it. When I reminded him of the rule, he replied that some of the old men chewed snuff. He was being assertive, masculine, and cynical, as he undoubtedly was justified in being.

Early in this summer, Fred, Jeff, a parallel cousin and his wife had gone to Bethel to trade. Jeff did the trading of oil and skins for both Fred and himself, but he kept separate account of his brother's products. Fred was quite pleased with the result of the trade, having received thirty dollars for a poke of seal oil and thirty dollars for each of the two mukluk skins that he had obtained the preceding spring. They had remained in Bethel about a week. Fred had not liked it.

After many hints and refusals to talk openly, Fred revealed that the only woman or girl who was attractive to him was a married woman with four children. He liked her because she was so clean. She was indeed unusually clean, energetic, and apparently above average intelligence. His love for her seemed hopeless, but he obtained from me small articles that he planned to give to her the following Christmas (anonymously, I presumed). I never was able to learn whether cleanliness in himself and others had the symbolic meaning that it has according to Western psychology.

Having heard that his foster sister, Barbara, and her own mother were uncongenial, I tried unsuccessfully to get Fred's attitude or information regarding the matter. He said he did not know and showed distaste for the subject. But when I told him that I thought Barbara was very cute (the term really fitted her), he grinned with pleasure. Evidently both he and Barbara resented their separation. Although Barbara had rejected Rose, her real mother, and had accepted Jane as her mother, she also was happy to be permitted to stay with Jeffrey and Fred the coming winter in order to attend school in Mekoryuk. That Mekoryuk was her original home and that she enjoyed school also influenced her. She made no plea to accompany Lewis and Jane when in the fall they returned to their home at Nash Harbor.

Barbara had not yet accepted Lewis as a father substitute. She charged that he had used for himself her earnings from her work at the Reindeer Project, which was not true. Also, one time while drawing a picture of a boat, she said, "My father's boat is good." I asked whether she meant Lewis's boat. She said, "No, Matthew's boat. Lewis's boat is no good."

Barbara gave constant evidence of her attitude toward her real and foster parents, in such conversations as these. One day I complimented her on her decorated old-style women's boots of gray sealskin and asked who had made them. When she replied, "Mother," I asked whether she meant Jane or Rose. She said, "Jane," her foster mother. Fred was not so fortunate: he no longer could claim any of his three foster mothers.

THE SHAMAN

RICHARD CHAPPEL

Ernest Norton, Interpreter

Richard was a rather boyish-looking man, not effeminate but simply younger looking than his years. (He was in his thirties.) He had an unaggressive manner and a disarming, deprecating smile. He was, however, a shrewd and stubborn trader in selling his ivory carvings, which were very good. He needed to be, as this was an important means of livelihood for him. He was a cripple and could not do all types of hunting, fishing, and trapping, although some were possible for him. His left leg was bent at the knee enough so that his foot never touched the ground in walking, always on crutches. His leg had stiffened in such a position that it twisted outward slightly. Richard lived in one of the dimmer and dingier underground houses with his wife and a young daughter adopted by his wife before this marriage. She had also more or less adopted a pleasant but moronic young man. Richard had been a shaman, but had ceased to practice after the missionary came.

1. I was born at St. Michael. I was the youngest—I had two older brothers. I had a sister, but she died at St. Michael. My father was a Nunivak man and my mother a Nelson Island woman. After we lived a few years at St. Michael, we returned to Nunivak, to Ka´nigiakhtuli´gamiut. We came in a schooner.

2. At St. Michael just before we came to Nunivak, I fell off a dock and hurt my leg, but not badly. I thought nothing of it. The first winter after I came back to Nunivak, my leg began to get bad—it twisted to one side. I have walked on crutches ever since then.

3. My mother died soon after we returned. I stayed with my father. Later he married again. My brothers never married. One

of my brothers was named Tunaga´likh [meaning "shaman"] but he never was really a shaman.

4. Three very important things happened to me within a year or two: my leg was hurt; I returned to Nunivak [where his father was disliked and feared]; and my mother died. I was about eight years old. I always have tried to live according to the old laws. I listened to what people told me. They told me to do these things:

5. People said a boy should not sleep long, should not sleep the whole night through. If he did not sleep a lot, he would catch seals and other game. He should never sleep outdoors in winter. He should never take toys outdoors in winter. I tried to stay awake, but I couldn't.

6. A boy should sweep out the entranceway of the kazigi. If he was industrious in this, he would see a little seal's head on the floor of the entranceway or feel the fur on a seal's back.

7. If a man went out from the kazigi and saw a little seal with a human face like this, with a feather sticking in its back, he should pull out the feather. It would help him become a good hunter. The little seal would disappear.

8. If a person when going outside the village sees a mass of worms, he should put his hand in an intestine, then put it on the worms. He must not be afraid. Then he can cure sickness: can put his hand on sickness and pull it out.

9. People should take care of the seal bones—should put them back in the sea.

10. Sometimes a person sees something big beckoning to him in the mountains. A person should go toward that thing. As he approaches, it gets smaller until it is the size of a forefinger, and it will have a leather thimble on it. A person should not be afraid. He should take it home and put it in a little bag with sewing or carving or something. In the morning the work will be finished. I wish I had such a thimble. [He smiled.]

11. Gregory's maternal grandmother once saw one. She went toward it a long way but never reached it. Even so, she became a very good seamstress—very quick. She could sew a whole kayak cover in one night. Such a thimble was called ta´qaGia´khchia.

12. When I was a boy at Ka´nigiakhtuli´gamiut, there was one kazigi. These families lived there: Simon, Sophie's father, Ki´oGan's father, Stephen's father, Thomas Scott's grandfather, Clarence Puguya´khtokh, and Lukhtusi´Gakh's father. Thomas' grandfather was called a wealthy man. Gregory's maternal grandfather was uki´skakh at one time. Later, Aaron was uki´skakh.

13. Ki´oGan's father and Ki´oGan were my serious partners.

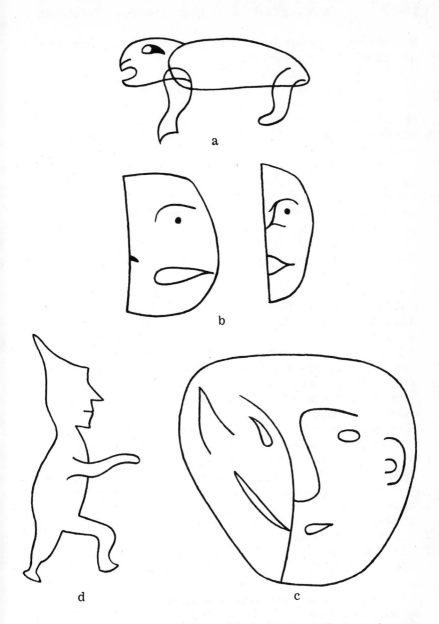

Figure 7. Drawings made by Richard while he talked, to illustrate the creatures that he mentioned: (a) frog used in divination; (b) "half people"; (c) half animal, half human spirit; (d) a man of the "little people." See pages 114, 116 and Notes.

Not only my father and my brothers had the same partners but also my father's brothers and their sons.

14. People also taught me that sometimes a man traveling sees a board hanging down from the sky by two ropes. He must not try to run around it or jump over it—it can move faster than he—he should crawl under it. Then Lam-chuakh will take him up and give him power to get lots of seals. I don't know of anyone who has seen such a board.

15. Sometimes a person will hear a "frog" in a wet place go "p'lup-p'lup-p'lup." This is a pla´qa-pla´Ga. If a man finds one and puts it inside his clothes and it crawls around his waist, all the way round, he will live long. If it goes around halfway, he will not live long. He should dry it and store it safely.

16. There are half-people, called i´Nalukaiyu´Gat. And i´khchit with two sides of the face different, maybe a man on one side and fox on the other.

17. Children still know about tukai´yuli ["little people"] and i´kh-chit today. But they take toys outdoors in winter and do other things that I didn't do when I was a boy. I always tried to live according to the rules.

18. When I was a boy, I was very frightened when the spirits came in the kazigi during the Bladder Feast. I did not know that the spirits were men until I was almost grown.

19. When I was grown, we moved to Nash Harbor. My father had died before this.

20. Sometimes when a boy went in the entranceway, he would see two other entrances. One went down underground, into darkness. If a person went down that entrance, he would not return. The other one above the real entrance led up into a house. If the boy went up, he would find a woman there. She would ask him if he wore his own clothes or borrowed clothes. If he said "my own clothes," he would not return; if he said "borrowed clothes," then he could return home.

21. People taught children not to eat outdoors in winter. A man out hunting could eat outdoors if there was no village he could go to.

22. After a young man caught a bearded seal for the first time, he had to wear his hood up over his head even indoors. He could not look up. At any time, young men hunting seals were warned not to sleep on the back because they should not look up. Lam-chuakh would punish people for doing these things.

23. If a man outside the village sees a big crack, he should fall

backward. If he doesn't fall back, he will fall down in the crack and be swallowed by the earth and never come back.

24. When I was young, only Constance's husband, Akha'LiNokh, lived at Paimiut. There were very few at Mekoryuk then. Only Joshua lived here. At Nash Harbor there were Norton family; Martha's father, James; Bob Wilson's father; Cook family; Dan Johnson's grandfather, Awi'giyakh; Cannon; Harmon; and Lewis.

25. This is the Bladder Feast at St. Michael as I remember it: They hung the bladders in three bunches at the back of the kazigi, not the same as on Nunivak. I am not sure about models of things hung up in the kazigi. I think not. I don't remember them. Here on Nunivak Island when I was young there was no ceremony to tell boys the real nature of the spirits. Boys found out by themselves. People told them the story of the Bladder Feast [i. e., the traditional story of its origin] from about seven years old. Then older boys [i. e., at adolescent age] usually told each other or each boy would notice by himself the true identity of the spirits.

26. Once, in my village, I saw four shamans have a contest to see which was strongest. The fourth one had people bind his arms and legs and tie rocks to his legs. People took up the boards above the fireplace, then took away the light. When they lighted the lamp again, he was on the opposite side of the fireplace.

27. Another shaman told the people to put a piece of antler up in the skylight—nail it there. Then he was tied like the other shaman. People put his drum in his mouth—the drum handle. Then they tied him to a pole with light sinew cord. They put out the light. When the lamp was lighted, the sinew cord that had been around him was now hanging down from the piece of antler even though the shaman had not moved.

28. The second man had people tie him so that he couldn't move. They put him in the entrance. They removed the light. When they put the light in again, he was untied and came in even though no one touched him.

29. The first shaman had people break his drum cover. He took the broken drum toward the entrance, put it in the entrance while the lamp was still lighted. People saw him do it. When he pulled the drum in again, it was whole, as before—not broken.

30. The one who hung sinew over the antler and the one who fixed his drum were considered the strongest.

31. In the kazigi once when people were having a festival, a shaman jumped up on the shelf, put on snowshoes and took two canes. He put on a gut parka. There were five witnesses, one of them a

young woman, and four healthy young men. The shaman told the five witnesses that when he went down in the entrance, they must chase him. He went toward the entrance slowly, slowly as he could. He went down in it slowly, wearing snowshoes. The witnesses watched closely. When the top of his head disappeared, they went out fast to chase him. They came in, told the people they could not see him or catch him. The woman said the shaman was up in the corner of the kazigi. She alone could see him. He was sparking. [Ernest: "Just like a sparkplug!"]

32. The shaman was going after the eclipsed moon. He waited—did not return while they sang three songs. Then he came in very slowly. People took hold of him, brought him in. They removed his clothes. He was very stiff, hardly moved. He was named Apaʹ-Gakh. He told the people that some other shaman had gone up before him and fixed the moon. ApaʹGakh did not reach the moon. He saw it had been fixed, so he came back, sadly.

33. If there was no shaman in the village, people prayed to their kiʹLkat and iʹnoGot to end an eclipse.

34. Any people, not just shamans, might pray to their kiʹLkat to bring illness or harm to others.

35. People believed that if the moon was eclipsed as it rose in the east, the people to the east would get sick and wouldn't live long. If it was eclipsed in the west, the same would happen to the people in the west. An eclipse might mean starvation, too. The moon-man has a dog with no hair, smooth as if shaved. There was no explanation of the cause of an eclipse. Nunivak people didn't know how it happened. Some shamans had the moon's dog as a helping spirit.

36. A shaman would train a young man to be a shaman for a year.

37. A young man saw spirits in his dreams. They just came to him in dreams. That's how he got his helpers. Also, he saw them when just traveling around. They trembled.

38. A Liʹkhkakh is a spirit, a ghost spirit. alaʹNagu: same as a Liʹkhkakh. An uʹmiuga-GaniʹuGan is a real person who talks against or causes trouble to another person, then the second one won't pay any attention to him.

39. This is a story of a big village on Nelson Island long ago: It had two chiefs. One of them had one child, a boy. The boy was sick. The two chiefs begged the shaman to cure the boy. He tried, but couldn't. One shaman was a poor man. People didn't know he was a shaman. He was very poor.

40. That poor man told the boy's parents they should put him in the kazigi. The poor man told the people to put the boy in front

of the lamp. They put a grass mat in the entrance. The shaman danced while the people sang. The boy died while he was dancing. That man told the people that if he went out and they saw something coming in, they should not make any noise. Even if they saw a bad thing, they should not cry out or make a noise. A Thing would come in. It would be the moon-dog. When the dog went out, two men should follow it.

41. People began to sing when the poor man went out. While they sang, a dog came in, with no hair. When he jumped, the people stopped the song. His ears were big and dropped down. The dog went to the child. People made a little noise, the dog became afraid, nearly went out. The dog ate the child from legs to head. He licked up even the blood of the child, clean as possible.

42. When the dog had finished, they yelled and the dog went out. Two men went out after him and found the child sitting on a grass mat, not sick any more. The two men brought the child into the kazigi so that people could see. They put the child on the floor and he went to his father and mother.

43. The poor man went after the child, got it, and cured it with the help of the moon-dog.

44. After that he cured another child with the help of the moon-dog. He did not put the child in the center of the kazigi but in a corner.

45. The shaman told the people the moon-dog would not cure people any more because if he tried to cure a third time, he would drop the child in the dirt of the entrance, not in the grass, and not in the center of the kazigi. That was the end of the power of the moon-dog.

46. I heard in St. Michael, when I was a child, that if a person heard outside a sound like a mosquito he must tell the shaman quickly. Then when the shaman heard it, he danced, trying to take the thing from the air with his hands. He would show the people a little woman or little man in his palm. That was a chu´chikh, a soul.

47. When a man dies, the chu´chikh comes out and wanders around. I never have heard about this here on Nunivak—about the soul making a little buzzing noise.

48. My father married Kusau´yakh's mother, UmGa´Gakh, after my mother died. He was married to her until I was in my teens. Then she died. When I was eighteen, my father married Lydia's mother. He was married to her four years. She died. Then he was married to Edwin Larson's present wife, AyaGa´Lagia, for one

year. Then my father died. He was named Kapu ´Gan. When my
father married Lydia's mother, there was only Lydia. She had
no other children.

49. I started "dreaming" when I was about as big as Arnold
[about eleven years old].

50. I was scared at first. But later I was not frightened at all.
I told my father that I was seeing things in my dreams. Father
told me not to tell anyone. I don't know whether my stepmother
ever knew about my dreams. I not only saw spirits in dreams,
I saw them when I was awake—everywhere. Any little object might
seem to be moving. That was its spirit making it move. I saw
things moving outdoors. But especially I saw things in my dreams.
I didn't know that others weren't having dreams like mine; I thought
everyone had such dreams; I took them for granted. I did not talk
about them. At night when all the men were asleep in the kazigi, I
would be awake. I would look up and see many people moving around
on the kazigi ceiling. Sometimes, when I looked at a branch of a
shrub, tiny people and even their dogs came out from the ends of
twigs.

51. When I saw these things, I trembled. I trembled very easily.
Whenever I heard a loud noise, I would start to tremble.

52. The first time I tried to cure someone, I didn't really know
how to doctor, but people asked me to do it. They put the sick man
in the center of the kazigi. I took my drum, I started to drum and
a new song came to me. And then another new song.

53. Songs would just come right out of things, from the rim of
the drum or the light of the lamp or a fire burning, or when I was
outdoors and a bird flew over: I would hear it singing a song.

54. That time, when I looked at the sick man, I saw two men:
the body of the man and his shadow right next to him. I didn't know
what this meant at first, but Edwin Larson's mother-in-law, who
was a shaman, told me that the shadow was the man's soul. When
a person is going to die, his soul starts to leave. I sang over him
and the man got somewhat better.

55. The man got worse again. I sang again, but this time when
I looked at the man, his shadow was entirely separated from his
body. He got a little better but I didn't try to cure him any more.

56. Later, in doctoring other people I used a gull feather to
brush away the sickness. (It was not a split feather. A split feather
vane was used only for sewing the kayak cover.) I also sucked out
disease. My father gave me a spirit for sucking out sickness and
a song to go with it.

57. Then one time, I—my spirit—went to get seals. I had a little

figure of a seal to guide me. I told young men to prepare rainparka, hunting hat, snowshoes, and a big ice hook. I am not sure about the hat, but they prepared several things for a journey. They made a hole in the ice. I went down under the ice and traveled to a different world. It was much like this world, but seemed far away, as when I see things in my dreams. It was like a dream.

58. I came out on shore—in that world—and went up to a kazigi. I found the little seal beside the entrance. I went into the entrance, looked up through the floor doorway. The people in that kazigi told me not to come in, to go back. So I returned. When I came back in my own kazigi, the little seal dropped down from the skylight. I was very tired from this journey.

59. Then one time people told me to do this way: put mats on the floor of the kazigi like this, five of them, with a lamp on each side and my drum in front of the rear mat. They put water boots and rainparka on me and put me on the mat at the rear. They told me— they told my spirit—to travel around to each of the mats and then go out. One old man told me I would go down to the shore. There, I would find a whale scapula. I must turn it over. Under it I would find a spotted seal. I must beat it and the seal would spit out many tomcods. Another old man said I should go on along shore. I would see an old man with a kayak in which were many tomcods. Another man said, if I went on, I would see a storehouse full of tomcods. My spirit traveled and saw things exactly as the old men had said.

60. After this journey, I was not tired but I was hungry. Usually after spirit journeys this was so.

61. The shaman's drum represented the world. By means of his drum, he traveled all around over the world. One time I put a little figure of a spider on my drum. That spider went up to the roof and then berries dropped down on the drum.

62. One time they told me to stop the winds. I made a circuit of the kazigi putting dry grass crosswise on the bench. I had a big ice dipper full of grass. I went clockwise to south, west, north, northeast, and southeast. Southeast was the strong wind, bad for Nunivak. It was too strong. I couldn't stop it.

63. The old men told me to pound in the corners of the kazigi as hard as I could. They said Nunivak was like this. One should pound to drive it down solidly into the earth.

64. One time I saw this happen, between two shamans. One came out from the village wearing an a´nsun in the way they used to do at the Messenger Feast. Another met him, with his arms through the sleeves of his parka but not wearing the parka—just had it spread in front of him. He spread his arms, the sleeves, out and brought

them together in front of him [like opening and closing of butterfly wings or flapping of bird wings]. The other shaman fell down, his spirit left him and traveled down under the earth. It came back and he got up. He started on, but the other shaman, still approaching him, again flapped the parka. The shaman fell down again, and his spirit traveled to the sky world. He said there were five worlds, one above another. They looked like this world, only far away. The second shaman didn't know that these things would happen to him.

65. I did all these things before I was married. When the church came, I became a Christian and tried to forget my dreams and spirits. But for three years I still saw spirits and saw things moving. When I looked outdoors, I could see places far away. Then after three years they left me. I have tried to be a good Christian—maybe all lies.

66. My serious partners are Ellen and Steve Ezra, Paul and Christine, Lucinda and Ethan's wife, Wilbert Daniel and his brothers and sister. But not Herbert Noga´takh even though he is a brother of Lucinda. I am a partner to these women through my mother and their mother. I am a cousin of Herbert, just a cousin, not a joking cousin. I think Herbert's father was a paternal uncle to my father, so Herbert and my father were cousins [i. e. , "brothers" in the Nunivak system].

COMMENTS

Two of the brothers had married two sisters: Richard and Chu-Na´Gakh married daughters of Russell. ChuNa´Gakh died, and the Eskimo missionary married his widow. Jessie had been married to Nicholas [See page 149] before she married Richard. Jessie was sick a long time before she died; in 1945 Richard's only child had died rather suddenly, before Jessie. She had had abdominal pain, "a very bad stomach-ache. " (Jessie probably had tuberculosis; her brother had been a tuberculosis patient in a hospital many months, and two sisters had died in recent years.) When Jessie died, Richard moved to Mekoryuk to marry Celia.

Ernest: Richard had been happy with Jessie, and he felt her death seriously. He was not happy with Celia now. Richard had told Ernest that if there were not a law against divorce nowadays, he would leave Celia. "He likes her well enough, " that is, she was sufficiently attractive to him sexually, and she took good enough care of the family, "but she doesn't care what she says. " She was irresponsible in her talk and said bad things about Richard, accusing him of things that were not true. (What bad things?) That was why he wanted to leave her. Ernest did not suggest that they quarreled openly. He said in a general way, "Husbands and wives don't quarrel the way they used to."

NOTES

1. Ernest: Richard's father had left Nunivak because he was afraid. He was a shaman and people accused him of doing harm to others and threatened to kill him.

2. There was no opportunity for a thorough physical examination of Richard, including X-ray, etc., to determine the nature of his leg ailment. It may well have been a contracture due to conversion hysteria. The circumstances in the original period of contracture and the twisted position of the leg suggest it. Or, it may have been due to tuberculosis of the bone, not at all uncommon in this area which has a high tuberculosis rate, or may have been other organic difficulty.

3. Unfortunately, I could elicit no more on his mother's death or father's remarriage.

Ernest: "He drowned; his body washed ashore after the family moved to Nash Harbor, later. In fact, both brothers drowned." The other brother was named ChuNa'Gakh, not mentioned at this time, and he did marry. It is significant that only the shaman brother—he tried to be a shaman—was mentioned. At this time, however, Richard was covering up his own shamanistic practice, apparently unaware that I already knew about it.

4. The defense, viz., that he had tried to live according to the laws, came immediately after the statement of the trauma. In his life, it had happened similarly: he had gone into a religious fantasy life soon after this period of undoubtedly great anxiety. The religious and magical practices with their promise of success, prestige, wealth must have represented a promise of security or just escape from reality. He must have wanted to get magical power to overcome his physical deficiency and also the social antagonism toward his father. Other factors may have been involved: he apparently had a good relationship with his father, at any rate better than the brother's relation to the father; hence he may have felt guilt for not having adequately followed his father's teaching and adequately supported him in an adverse world. If he admired his father's power and knowledge of the supernatural and identified with him, Richard probably was describing actually his relation

to his father even though consistently using impersonal terms. Or, if "the people" who gave instruction on getting power were all the old men forming the kazigi community and not only or primarily his father, he may have turned to religion in an effort to identify with them. Possibly, like the community, he disliked and feared his father in a genuine ambivalence (dependence and resistance). In any case, he felt guilt for something and shamanism was his compensation and defense.

7. That he could travel and go hunting (alone in a kayak and occasionally alone on a sled) shows his adequate self-assurance, the economic necessity, and the force of the culture, in which every man had to be a hunter. But he never had been a good hunter and probably felt inferior on that score even though he had a good physical excuse and quite good emotional defense. He did not show the discomfort, the open anxiety about hunting that some others showed.

10. This was a reference to his abundant ivory carving, which was carefully made and technically very good although somewhat rigid in style and stereotyped in subject.

12. I asked who lived in his village, in an effort to get his attention back to his own childhood, especially his personal relationships.

Uki´skakh meant the man with highest social and economic position, not a political office.

13. Richard still was not ready to talk about his personal relationships; also, he seemed not much interested in them. His emotion centered on religious teaching and experience. He probably was not just inhibiting but was repressing into the subconscious his real feelings. The last statement was said as if answering a question from me. He knew that I accepted his and other people's visions, but I would ask questions regarding people who had had such experiences, as a matter of personal interest.

15. See Fig. 7(a). Ernest: "Maybe it's used for curing." This form of divination, not strictly curing, has been reported from the Upper Yukon and the Lower Kuskokwim.

16. See Fig. 7(b) and (c).

17. See Fig. 7(d). Ernest, a Christian lay preacher, said he believed in tukai´yuli and i´khchit. Sometimes he heard the tukai´-yuli, little people, knocking.

I had asked three times, at intervals, regarding any epidemics or other misfortunes on the island that he knew about when he was a boy. His only answer was to tell about the tabus, implying that if people did not act right, they would get sick, the general local view.

Did he feel that he was crippled because of something his father or
he had done? Perhaps his father had killed people with magic? Or,
was this merely an illustration of the common local idea that one
must not talk of sickness, else sickness will come? Incidentally,
Nunivakers are not hypochondriac. Or, did he need to avoid the
subject consciously? His mother may have died in an epidemic.

20. His insistent return to the same topic suggests either a compulsion neurosis or that he had decided before the interview to talk
only about these supposedly impersonal teachings. That he did talk
more freely in later interviews can substantiate either supposition
(1) that he got relief and was able to go on less compulsively or (2)
that he thought the matter over and decided he could talk more personally. But he never responded freely or directly to my questions.
I suspect he was compulsive, that at the point in his life which he
was discussing, he was concerned with these teachings because
he had a great anxiety, expressed in his fear of being lost, being
swallowed up in the crack, or in the underground passage. His
massive anxiety, his fear, became focused on Lam-chuakh, the
great Sky Deity who punishes one for breaking the tabus mentioned
and for other sins. Later the religious teachings became part of
a pleasurable system when he had learned to cope with his difficulties. He had enjoyed being a shaman. Ernest said Richard's
father, like other shamans, had lots of spirits, animal spirits and
others, to help him. He was certain that Richard still believed in
these things.

24. Ernest said he himself was thirty-two years old (thirty-four
years, according to church and school records) and he knew that
Richard was older (thirty-six years, according to records). Regarding adults, however, there was no certainty in any statements
or records pertaining to age. The period referred to here was
twenty-five to thirty years earlier.

25. Ernest said he had asked Richard what his principal helper-
spirit was or what some of his spirits were. Richard would not
tell him (even though both nominally were Christian and supposedly
no longer believed in old spirits). Ernest commented that shamans
couldn't tell of their own spirits or powers.

The explanation about learning the identity of spirits in the Bladder Festival came in answer to a question.

26. I had asked Richard previously to tell about shamans' performances and shaman contests that he had seen. He had ignored
the subject. Now he evidently had thought about it, decided to tell
me. He answered the opening questions regarding the Bladder
Feast, then voluntarily began to describe shaman seances.

34. Explanation in answer to question.

36. Ernest: Richard's eldest brother wanted to be a shaman and tried to be, but claimed his father took his spirits away from him.

37. Ernest: "They trembled like figures in the old movies."

38. Does this mean, distrusts him and won't believe anything that he says or becomes estranged, won't have any dealings with him?

39. Richard stressed the poverty of the shaman and the fact that the village did not know that he was a strong shaman. Richard undoubtedly identified himself with the shaman of the tale.

47. There was a similar, although not identical, concept. Richard probably sought exactness of belief and practice, the "right way."

48. In this interview, I asked Richard two series of questions (1) regarding family relationships, his father's marriages, his stepmothers and stepsiblings; (2) his own experiences as a shaman. On the first, he said as little as possible; on the second, he talked quite freely. Reasons: (1) as child and young man, he probably had tried to ignore everyday family relations, which were unpleasant, we can safely guess. He evidently lived in a dream world; his spiritual experience was more satisfying. (2) He had made up his mind to tell me about his shaman powers, about which Ernest and I had asked him previously. Richard offered to come and talk. (He may have needed the money, too.) Apparently Richard's father did not have children by any of the women mentioned. If Lydia was the only stepsibling, it is understandable that Richard would not talk about her: she was younger than he and his brothers. This marriage to Lydia's mother must have occurred when Richard was learning to be a shaman, probably paying no attention to anyone but himself. Even so, his avoidance of reference to his family is significant: he at no time referred to his brothers drowning. He did not talk about his own marriage. Ernest obviously hesitated to ask, Richard's first wife having died only the year before.

49. This was only a couple of years after he became lame or perhaps when his leg was still in the process of contracting. However, the latter seems to have occurred rather quickly.

50. Facial expression indicated that he enjoyed it.

51. Ernest: "Shamans always did this."

54. The woman shaman was not at that time Edwin Larson's mother-in-law but was the mother-in-law of Richard's father, hence stepgrandmother to Richard. If the order of Richard's father's marriages given in the interview is correct (which it may not be) Richard was twenty-two or twenty-three years old when this occurred. According to Ernest, Richard's father married

AyaGa´Lagia, Edwin's present wife, then later married UmGa´-Gakh. If this is true, then Richard was sixteen or seventeen years old when this incident occurred.

56. Because an older shaman had mentioned such a feather, I asked about it. Richard's answer shows the variation in shamanistic practice.

58. Richard seemed entirely sincere. I suspect that his father and stepgrandmother fixed up the little seal. Ernest: People who had seen this had told him about it. The little seal image had hair on it when it returned.

59. Richard's sketch of the arrangement of mats has been lost. Every time he described his visions, he narrowed his eyes and looked out the window, with a faraway look. Previously I had noticed him doing this, sitting very still while others talked around him. His expression at such times generally was peaceful, not tense or unhappy.

62,63. He did not offer the traditional explanation of stuffing the mouth of the wind with grass although this probably was the basis of the action. It is not at all clear that Richard understood what he was doing. He seems to have done what he was told without always knowing why. In some shamanistic matters, perhaps no one understands any longer, for example, the reference to the moon-dog after the discussion of an eclipse. Richard did not indicate that a dog had anything to do with an eclipse, as is commonly believed.

64. A´nsun was a large mask, often in the form of a tall pointed head.

The final statement of the paragraph was made in answer to a question: whether the second shaman knew that the first might send him on journeys.

65. Ernest: Other shamans had trouble giving up their spirits, too. Some of them got sick, like Helene Stephen. (See Helene's biography.) Richard seemed to have no fear of charges of sorcery, as Helene had. According to one woman, most people thought that he did not have much power and did not fear him. Also, he probably had practiced innocently, not aware of all the trickery. To the end, he would not tell what his helping spirits were, showing that he did not think they were lies. The last phrase was said in English, with a smile.

66. Richard told willingly, even proudly, who were his partners. The partnerships were maintained despite some avoidance of his father by the community. It is difficult to tell, though, how well the obligations were observed.

THE WOMAN SHAMAN AND HER FAMILY

HELENE STEPHEN

Ernest Norton, Interpreter

Helene was one of the three last practicing shamans on the island, and accounted a strong one. She was not an old woman, however. When she gave this information about herself, she was said to be about forty-five. She had the reputation of being quarrelsome and dominating. To an outsider, her most noticeable trait was her frequent lack of poise, of the calm self-possession that is characteristic of most Nunivakers. She would fidget, appear embarrassed, become hesitant in speech, occasionally dart off when spoken to in the presence of others. At times she would appear as self-conscious and ill at ease as an inexperienced young girl, at other times she would be calm and entirely self-possessed.

She showed great motherly affection for her daughter, young adopted son, and small granddaughter (daughter's child), but the affection was possessive. She was a good seamstress, made beautiful parkas and boots, and gave adequate physical care to her family. Helene was plump and hearty, not the thin, tense type one might imagine from the above description.

1. The first thing I remembered, I was crying. I saw my own mother nursing my brother. I was crying because I wanted my mother to suckle me. And my mother did take me and suckle us both at the same time. My brother was younger.

2. Then I remembered nothing more for a long time. Next time I remembered, I was barefooted. I saw a woman, Joel's mother, who was married then to Scott's brother, Kali Gamiun. I don't know what happened—I forgot again.

3. Next time, I was in the kazigi. I saw Asael Sharp wearing a beaded band around his head and in his lip a big blue bead. Another

man was dressed the same. My brother gave me water to drink from a wooden bucket. The people had a feast. Someone came in: Benson and his aunt. I was living then at Mekoryuk. Years after that, I asked who the strangers were. They told me Benson and the others were from Nash Harbor. Spread all around inside of the kazigi were fish nets. Two men were dancing with the big "trays" [bearing little models of kayaks, animals, etc.]. Then I remembered no more.

4. Next I remembered, I was on the stairs of the entranceway. I went out and saw another entrance with a woman coming out of it. It was Luther's wife with a child about the size of Viola [two years old]. She said the child was my serious-partner. At that time, I didn't know that Richard Lewis' mother and other people were my partners.

5. Next time: I was at a Bladder Feast, up on the bench of the kazigi. I went to sleep and fell off. A man took me to the woman's house [i.e., family home]. I was wearing a white fox parka. He put me beside my foster mother. I cried because I wanted to go back to the kazigi, so the man took me back. I don't remember when my foster mother adopted me.

6. Next time: I was outdoors. I saw many people walking in the lagoon. They were gathering smelts—I found out when I went to them. From then on, I remembered everything. My own mother was living but I was adopted by someone else. I knew this then. I knew that my own father was Daniel. We moved to Cape Etolin to camp. My own mother and stepfather were there. The grown people did not tell me that I had my own mother and father, but my brother and sister told me. So I did what my brother told me to do and I went to my own mother. I was living with my foster mother, who was my mother's sister, but one day I went to see my own mother. I saw something black on the ground; I thought it was a bad spirit and returned as fast as I could. Then I saw Russell wearing a rain parka, and I found out Russell had put something to scare me, to keep me from going to my mother. Even though he did this, I continued going to my own mother. Every day I went to my mother, but one day my mother had gone somewhere and I did not see her any more.

7. When I was that age, I was always playing. When I got bigger, I was always going out in a kayak. One day I tipped over, at the mouth of the river near Mekoryuk. From then on, I knew I might tip over and I was more careful. One time we went upriver to get humpback salmon. My older sister told me to go back to the village. My older sister disliked me. She scolded me, so I said I

saw a bad spirit. I knew I was lying—I just said that to fool my sister. My sister believed me! I went back to the village. I was over ten years old at that time, but I don't know just how old I was.

8. One time my parents told me to get some water in the evening. I went out even though it was very dark. I was afraid but I reached the pond and took water. I had no light. The old village was at the other end of Mekoryuk (at the point); when I went past it, something whistled. I said nothing about it, I went in the house and went to sleep. The next day I went to see what kind of thing had whistled. I found a skull half buried in the ground. I dug it out and found it was very old. I threw it in the water. From then on, I dreamed, and saw things moving. I never was afraid of such things any more. Should I tell more?

9. I did not marry even though I was grown now [had reached puberty]. Sometimes, when I was alone in the house, the wall opened and I saw many things. I could see far through the wall.

10. In the morning when I woke up, I went to the entranceway and saw under the ocean (down in the entrance). I couldn't go back to my place on the bench. When a person walked through the entranceway, I went toward him and did not see under the ocean any more. Whenever I saw something like this, I trembled. When I told about seeing these things, my aunt told me not to tell anyone. I was living with my mother's sister. There were six of us, brothers and sisters—we were divided up. Some lived with my aunt, some with other people.

11. One time I dreamt about a tiny man. When I awoke, I saw a big man in a vision. Then I saw a large skeleton. I couldn't move.

12. After many years, I was married to Stephen. After I was married, I trembled whenever I heard a noise. Sometimes I would faint. So other people made me a drum. Although I was ashamed, I performed shamanism when people told me I should do it. After many years, I was sorry about having spirit helpers when I knew there was a "better way." I tried to go away from the spirits, but for a long time they went with me. Now I've lost most of them. Tell more?

13. People used to say that sickness is dark, like night, but I don't believe this now. I don't tremble any more, and I'm thankful.

14. I had a wooden doll when I was little, named pamu´Lagia (it means, frame of kayak). I used to make clothes of puppy skins for it.

15. I lived at Ka´nigiakhtuli´gamiut when I was first married (to Stephen). He came there to live with me. At my first menstruation, I was not married yet. I did not have to stay in a separate hut be-

cause I wasn't married yet. I was not frightened. One time I saw a man and woman in a snow hut. I saw a light under the snow, so I knew they were in a hut [covered by a snowdrift] because of the wife's first menstruation.

16. My aunt told me not to eat fresh fish—that was the first rule. I had no grass around my wrists and ankles, although once I saw a man and wife whose child had died, and they were wearing grass like this. Once, in a Bladder Feast when I went to get mukluk I wore grass around my ankles. It was like a dream. The hole in the ice was like an entranceway. Under the sea it was like this world. The animals lived in little camping places. When I came to such a village, I went into the entrance of the kazigi. I found it was very deep with a round step (a round stone or something of the kind). A little boy came out from the kazigi. He would not let me go in; he told me not to go in.

17. I found two trails when I went. I went under the sea on the right one, and came back on the left trail. When I returned toward my own village, I saw three villages, on three levels. I went to the middle village. People sang a new song when I went on this journey. They sang another new song when I came back, a song composed by Herbert's father. I could not go in the kazigi because I was very tired. Two people helped me in from the entrance to the kazigi. When Rhoda [her daughter] was the size of Viola [two years old], this happened. Then two men told me to get up on the bench. I lay down and rested because I was very tired. Then I went into the woman's house.

18. Next day, old people told me to put grass around my ankles. I fasted one day and I did not work. I wore mittens. From the beginning of winter (i. e., Bladder Feast) until spring I did not eat fresh foods and no seal, not even oil. I did not want to eat the food other people were eating. From the Bladder Feast on, I drummed every day until spring. That was my first journey. Then people told me to get spotted seals and all kinds of seals.

19. When spring came, the people told me to pull the oogruk over to Nunivak. For three days after pulling in the oogruk, I did not drum. People caught a lot of seals, but I did not eat seal because when I went on a journey to get seals, I had seen people. Seals were just like people.

20. After that, although people asked me to get animals, I didn't like to do it because I got tired. I did not want to practice shaman powers any more at that time.

21. A woman shaman taught me what to do. But without being taught, I knew about the hole in the ice that was like an entrance-

way and about the trails under the ice. When I went to the hole in the ice, there was no water under the ice. It was just like a world.

22. Do you think that I used my spirits against people? I am afraid people will think that I have.

COMMENTS

Important aspects of Helene's later married life were not included in her story. It appears that she introjected her mother. She became a compulsive mother, doing as much as she could for her family according to her conception of maternal duty, because she had lacked such a mother.

Stephen was a good husband for her. He became a well-to-do hunter, providing more than adequate economic security. He appeared quiet, stable, unaggressive, permitting her to dominate the family.

Helene's daughter, Rhoda, was a pretty girl, socially immature. At this time she and her husband were living apart—for the twelfth or thirteenth time, he claimed. Periodically she fled home to her mother. She seemed to spend most of her time by herself, pouting. Her husband, unfortunately, also came from a family with personality problems. He was a tense, excitable young man. But they loved each other and were reunited.

NOTES

1. Both Ernest, interpreter, and Helene's half sister, Rachel, said that Austin, the brother referred to, was older than she. But according to the order of the mother's marriages (she and her daughters had complicated marital histories) and the recognized paternity of her children, Helene was right in saying that her brother was younger. In any case, the brother was taking her place as the baby of the family. Helene avowed a childhood sibling rivalry more openly than any others who told their stories. This little scene establishes the theme of her childhood perfectly: she had to fight to have a mother.

2., 3. These scenes probably are remembered for some action, the memory of which she has repressed.

5. It is noticeable that she specifies "foster mother."

6. Daniel revealed in his autobiography that he had deserted A´naGaN, Helene's mother, when she was pregnant, carrying a female foetus, but he did not say that that girl child was Helene or that his wife had had three children before marrying him. His complete omission of any reference to these stepchildren, who must have been quite young, is remarkable.

Helene lost her fight to have a mother. The mother, too, undoubtedly was having difficulties at this time. In such a crucial period, Helene's learning that spirits could be used for human purposes or could be alleged when they did not exist may have helped prepare her for a career as a shaman.

7. She did not tell which sister was referred to here. She had two older half sisters, one being the Ko´nakosiN mentioned by Christine, the woman who was married to Masoa´lokh and then to his father. The other was Rachel, whose account is given below. This incident in which Helene used the spirit against her sister evidently seemed as significant to Ernest Norton as to me, because at this point he said to me, "Helene will not tell everything about her life."

8. This agrees with Richard Chappel's statement that there was a point in his experience with the spirits at which he lost his fear of them. From that point onward, both he and Helene obviously enjoyed their visions. Probably Helene felt the experience more intensely and suffered more because she was a more completely rejected child than he: her real father and mother deserted her; her foster father was barely mentioned and apparently meant nothing to her; her foster mother was inadequate; and she said—as if it were undeniable—that her older sister disliked her. Helene

struggled to protect herself and gained the strength to overcome the skull spirit.

10. At about this point, she asked the interpreter, "Should I tell even about my shame?" referring to her adultery early in her marriage. He said, "Yes." Then she asked, "Should I tell even about being a shaman?" He said, "Yes." She did not, however, tell about the former but did tell of the latter. From here on, she was obviously very disturbed, and needed prompting and reassurance. She ceased trying to give an organized, chronological account.

14. To get away from the situation that had developed, which must have seemed to her a demand that she confess guilt, to give her a chance to relax a bit, I asked her questions on more impersonal matters: her games and playthings, where she had lived, the tabus that she or other girls had had to observe at puberty. There is no personal significance in her reference to puppy skins: these were commonly used for babies' parkas.

16. She voluntarily returned to the subject of shamanism, telling of it this time with somewhat greater ease and greater fullness of description. For one thing, she had seen that I did not censure her in any way, that, instead, I accepted and was sympathetic to the old beliefs and acts.

17. Ernest tried to clarify this account. He said Helene was married first to Stephen. After about two years, he left her. Then she married Clarence Puguya'khtokh. When she was pregnant by him, not long before the birth of Rhoda, Clarence left her, and very soon she went back to Stephen. Thus she got her drum and had some shamanistic practice when she was married to Stephen the first time. This first big journey to get mukluk (bearded seals) occurred when she was married to him the second time, in Rhoda's infancy. Greater sexual freedom generally was expected of a shaman than of a layman, yet Helene's personality difficulties, unfaithfulness, and threatening spirit-powers must have been too much for her young husbands. Whether she was unfaithful in her second marriage to Stephen was not ascertained.

18. This is the clearest evidence obtained that the shaman novice was thought to be unclean and had to go through an initiation period, as when a young man killed an oogruk and a girl reached puberty.

20. It is likely that both Stephen and Helene had tuberculosis, partially explaining her fatigue. But whether or not she had t. b., her emotional disturbance could have accounted adequately for her fatigue.

21. Her half sister, Rachel, said that she was taught shamanism

by the famous woman shaman, Icha´ganin, mentioned by both Daniel
and Christine. In the thick ice grounded on the beaches, the "fast
ice," it was possible to have a hole under the ice in which there
was no water at low tide. In a trance and enclosed in such a hole,
Helene undoubtedly had these visions.

22. Helene had a compounded guilt, in terms of both old and new
cultures. According to the old culture, she was guilty because she
and her sister were quarrelsome and aggressive and because she,
like all shamans having strong spirit-powers, was charged with
witchcraft. In the new culture, she was guilty of sexual offense
and of the mere practice of shamanism, no matter how well-meant.
Significantly, the only one that she stated directly to me—and the
one that probably disturbed her the most, subconsciously—was use
of her spirit-powers to harm others. Even if she never had used
them against others deliberately, she probably had *wanted* to use
them that way. She had acquired the powers in the first place in
order to fight a community that must have seemed hostile to her.

RACHEL

Ernest Norton, Interpreter

Rachel was a rather pretty woman, with a pleasing low soft voice, and gave a superficial impression of being a sweet woman. She had, however, the reputation of being difficult to get along with. She had what appeared to be a wart under the septum of her nose that was said to have been caused in a quarrel years before when her husband grabbed her string of nose beads and pulled them, breaking through the septum of her nose. Also, she and Sophie, her young married daughter with whom she lived, quarreled and separated every few weeks. Besides Sophie, only one child was still living: Arthur, thirteen or fourteen years old. Rachel was not married at this time.

I did not try to get more than impressions and information to supplement Helene's autobiography. Helene had fidgeted and squirmed through most of her interview, but Rachel was calm and able to speak objectively about such things as family relationships. She suppressed, though, one piece of information that was contrary to Christian morality.

1. First thing I can remember now, I was living at Ka´nigiakhtuli´gamiut with my mother and mother's sister. My father died and people pulled him up through the skylight. But I didn't understand then that that man was my father.

2. Next thing I remember, I was living at Mekoryuk with my mother. At the Bladder Feast, in the kazigi entrance I saw one of the spirits. I was frightened. I learned a long time later that it was Kiogoyu´Gakh. But I didn't know who the spirits were then— I was grown before I found out.

3. There were five children in my family, in order: Nai´Gakh,

Ko´nakosiN, myself, Ilu´waGa´Lagia (Austin), and Helene. Helene had a different father, Daniel.

4. Then I lived with my foster mother who was my mother's sister, Chu´qa, who was married to Kiogoyu´Gakh. My aunt adopted me and raised me. My own mother lived in the same village but I never lived with her.

5. Then my family (aunt and uncle) moved to Nash Harbor. At that time I thought Kiogoyu´Gakh was my own father. Nobody lived at Nash Harbor then except Harmon and James (Chani´ko´guyakh). In the spring we moved to Tachi´gamiut. Once when we children were sliding on a hill, we broke the sled. I and the others were hurt.

6. In summer we moved to Ati´Namiut for fishing. One day when I went out to get water, a young white fox barked at me and came and played with me. It was black [dark gray?] in summer.

7. In the summertime, I played all summer. Mostly we played ball, with a grass ball.

8. Next winter Chani´ko´guyakh and my foster father moved to Mekoryuk. They gave a dance (chuko´ka´galutiN). We had fun.

9. After that, some time, I was married to Nacha´galukh, Asael Sharp's brother. I was afraid. I had not known that I was going to be married. Then he left me.

10. Several years later when I was about the size of Betsy or a little younger [in late teens], I married an old man, Kiawi´Gakh. I was not afraid this time. I had four children from him, three boys and a girl. We traveled around, lived several places [mentioned four or five rapidly], but we lived principally at Naga´Gamiut.

11. My husband died in the flu epidemic when many people died. Then I was not married for a long time. Then, when I was not married, I gave Sophie to Benson to adopt, and I kept the other three children. Sophie was about the size of Sammy [i. e., about three years old] when I gave her away.

12. Then I married Nicholas's father, TaLi´likh, a mainland man. I had two children from him: Arthur and another boy before him, who died. Arthur was the last. At that time, TaLi´likh's son, Nicholas, was married to May, and his daughter, ANi´lan, was married to Aaron.

13. I was sort of afraid when I married TaLi´likh [because he was a shaman]. But he was a good man, he didn't hurt anybody. Then he died.

14. Then I married ANa´sakh who died before long. Finally I married Aaron, after ANi´lan died [1940]. Aaron left me and married Ethan's mother.

NOTES

1. Others besides Rachel made statements like these, indicating that in later years they discussed early childhood experiences, trying to identify people and occasions, or else they noted the stories told by their elders, trying to link their own memories to them. There was not so much error in either process as one would expect because these people had an objective interest in events: they valued good observation and reporting.

3. I asked her to name her siblings. There is evidence that Austin was younger than Helene despite Rachel's statement. Although she mentioned Helene's father, she failed to identify Austin's father. See below.

5. She did not tell about being hurt until I questioned her.

9. She must have been quite young, possibly only twelve years old.

10. The probable reason for Rachel's not mentioning Austin's father was this: this "old man," Kiawi´Gakh, married Rachel's and Helene's mother, then married Rachel, too, and lived with both of them simultaneously, according to others' statements. Austin was his son. I did not ascertain how long after these marriages her mother died. By the old-time code, there was nothing wrong in such a form of polygyny; but probably because Rachel knew it was wrong according to Christian teaching, she suppressed the information.

11. She did not mention that two of her three boys died when young, many years previously. Her failure to mention what had happened to a third son is understandable, since he had died only a couple of years before and she probably still mourned his death. She told about Sophie in answer to my question. I asked when Benson adopted Sophie, trying to phrase the question as impersonally as possible. Even so, she was somewhat perturbed and self-conscious when telling of "giving away" Sophie. This need not be attributed entirely to a feeling of guilt. She must have surmised that I had heard about her quarrels with Sophie and she was disturbed regarding her whole relationship to her daughter. Ernest Norton said that the flu epidemic did not hit Nunivak until about 1923 and that Sophie was born during the epidemic, just about the time her father died. Sophie was indeed born about 1924 but whether the big epidemic occurred then is not so certain. There is some evidence that Ernest was correct, that it was 1920-21, rather than 1918-19, when the epidemic reached the island. It must have

been hard for Rachel to care for her young children when she had no husband.

12. When she said that Arthur was her last child, her tone was quite regretful.

13. This was said in answer to a question. I asked whether Ta-Li'likh's possession of spirit-powers made any difference in her feeling for him.

14. Although she may have pitied herself because of her marital difficulties, her tone did not suggest that. Rachel reacted rather dully. Sophie was quick, responsive, and appeared quite intelligent. Rachel, in contrast, either was not so bright or else was so unhappy and inhibited that she could not react to her full mental capacity. She seemed to be unimaginative and did not see the other person's viewpoint. Her youngest child, Arthur, also appeared unaggressive, self-protective, passively negativistic, probably of only average intelligence. He put forth so little energy that it was difficult to judge him: his usual reaction was to smile, rather cynically, and do nothing. Very likely his mother was too dominating and possessive; and his only close attachment (to Louis Benson, another boy who was shy and ineffectual in the terms of Nunivak culture) suggested a latent, not overt, homosexual tie, as a substitute for the usual affectional relationships.

LYDIA

Charlie Sharp, Interpreter

Whenever family relationships were given, Lydia was stated to be the daughter of Ko'nakosiN and Ta'nnagikh or the niece of Helene Stephen. From two circumstances it seems likely that she was actually the daughter of Masoa'lokh, to whom her mother was married before marrying Ta'nnagikh: (1) Lydia named her eldest son Masoa'lokh, and her second son TaLi'likh for his paternal grandfather. The elder boy probably was named for his maternal grandfather, according to common Nunivak usage. There may have been some religious reason for the naming, yet there is the implication that Ta'nnagikh did not mean much to Lydia. (2) By several means of computing her age, she was about twenty-nine years old at this time, hence must have been born before or about the time of Masoa'lokh's death.

Hans, young Masoa'lokh, had been adopted by Stephen and Helene despite the tears of Lottie, eldest child of Lydia and Nicholas. Neither Lydia nor Nicholas indicated how they had felt. The reason cited for the adoption was that Stephen needed a son to help him in his later years. Helene, a forceful woman and a shaman who was feared, also may have intimidated Lydia and adduced her authority as aunt and her greater economic ability to care for Hans, who had been adopted when only a year old or less.

Lydia's manner was definite and strong, but pleasant and well balanced. She was a good worker and noticeable for being unusually clean. Her house and children also were kept clean although her adopted child, Davy, son of Lydia's uncle Austin, was neither fed nor clothed so well as her own children. He had been adopted in recognition of a family duty; he had not been getting good care in another foster home and Lydia had felt that she should take him away from that home, and also because she needed household help. It was customary to adopt poor orphan boys to get a slavey. Among

143

her own children, Lottie, about twelve years old, was a dependent girl, her mother's companion; Norbert seemed subnormal, perhaps because of deafness or other disability; and Ella was an indulged infant of two years.

1. The first thing I remember was my father's (Ta´nnagikh's) death. My family was living at Ka´nigiakhtuli´gamiut. I remember they ground up tobacco, put it beside his body. They laid his body on the ground and put things around him. That was the first time I had seen a dead person. I was the size of Melissa [about five and a half years old].

2. Next thing I remember is my mother telling me that I should dance at the Bladder Feast. I didn't want to—I think I was lazy—but I did dance.

3. Then there is another gap, a time that I don't remember. Then I remember that my mother married a medicine man (Kapu´-Gan). He was very dangerous and I was afraid of him. Also he didn't treat me well; he didn't take good care of me. We still lived at the same village after my mother married him.

4. Then we moved to Cape Manning. For the first time, I saw Charlie Sharp's family and others at Kani´khligamiut. John Lukhtusi´Gakh's family lived there and I played with John's children, Joel and Jane. (They were a little older than I was.) Things that happened at Cape Manning that I remember: I saw a man with a wolf tail on the back of his parka, first time I had seen a wolf tail or had seen a parka made that way.

5. Daniel's family lived there, too. In the spring, Daniel caught a mukluk. The boys raced out to him to get meat or blubber as they always did. Daniel ran to the village in the usual way and met me running out by myself. He stopped to play with me!

6. Next thing I remember, I was in a wooden boat with my family over by Nelson Island cliffs. The boat had belonged to my father (Ta´nnagikh), not to Kapu´Gan. We went to Tununak. I wondered at the different way people talked there. I played with the children. I went with a little girl through the village and saw a diamond necklace—real diamonds—but did not take it. When I went back to my mother, I told her about the diamonds. I said I wanted them. My mother told me not to take them, and I never saw them again.

7. Next: we were back at Ka´nigiakhtuli´gamiut. My family moved out to a fish camp in the summer. I found a young crane and brought it home. I fed it lots, I fed it everything, and it grew some. Then

for a little while I forgot to feed it, and it died. Later I caught other young birds and raised them: a tern, a sea gull, and others. They grew big and flew away.

8. In this period, my father used the drum, danced, called his spirits. Sometimes he wore a rain parka when he performed. After he had been using the drum, he would speak English. (At other times, he did not talk English.) People did not hear the spirits answer, or see them. He said they answered when he talked to his spirits.

9. From here on I remember everything year by year.

10. One evening when I was about eight years old [must have been older], I was very sleepy. My mother woke me and put a new parka on me. Several women were in the house. My mother gave me a dish with food, told me to take it to the kazigi and give it to Stephen's brother, Na'uwaGakh. This meant I was going to marry Na'uwaGakh. I hadn't known anything about it before this. I didn't like him and would not have anything to do with him. I was cross and cranky, I would not smile at him although he moved his things to my family's house. I never had intercourse with him. After a little while, he went away.

11. Then I was married to Gregory, who gave me cloth for a cloth over-parka. But I didn't like him, either. I would not sleep with him and he went away, too. I still have a piece of cloth from that cloth parka. My family did not give back the presents [parkas] to my husbands. My parents asked me to marry, told me I should. I said no, and they did not ask me again.

12. My mother died; then soon afterward, my stepfather died. My older stepbrothers, Richard Ka'Nalikh's older brothers, took the responsibility for me.

13. Then I married Nicholas. Nicholas asked my older brother for me. But this was not like the other marriages—I knew Nicholas wanted me because he was courting me as well as asking my brother. However, I ran away, left Nicholas after I was married to him a little while. He came and got me, though, and I stayed with him the second time.

14. That was all of my childhood.

NOTES

1. Lydia laughed a little in telling about the tobacco and other grave goods, knowing that this is not done in the new culture. The body probably was laid in a very shallow grave covered with rocks and boards. In her adulthood her father's (or stepfather's) death did not seem to her to have been a bad experience. Yet she evidently remembered it vividly.

3. Either she remembered less than others or else she was selecting, consciously or unconsciously, from her memories. Kapu´Gan was Richard's father.

4. There were no wolves on Nunivak in her lifetime, but wolf fur has been for some time obtained on the mainland by trade. Also in 1939-40, several boys and youths were seen wearing wolverine or other large tails on the back of the parka. Trade or style must have changed since her childhood, or else this parka represented wealth and good clothing which others had but which she lacked.

5. Daniel was a vigorous mature hunter at that time. There are several possible reasons why his stopping to play with her impressed Lydia so much: (1) ritual requirements may have been so strict that the interruption of a ritual duty was unlikely; (2) men may have taken little note of small girls, which seems improbable. Today, adults fondle any small children; (3) most likely, Lydia was alone and unnoticed generally, because of the community prejudice against her stepfather, because of her poverty and physical neglect, and the fact that she was a little girl in a family of boys, undoubtedly a lonely little girl. See below.

6. She gave a vivid description subsequently of the glass beads that she thought were diamonds or that she later thought must have been diamonds.

7. Best evidence of her loneliness was her bringing home and caring for birds, rather unusual behavior for a girl.

8. She gave this information about the spirits in answer to my question. It indicates that Kapu´Gan was not a ventriloquist.

10. She undoubtedly underestimated her age in justification of her resistance to marriage. She probably was eleven years old (see Richard Chappel's autobiography). It was obvious that she still felt strongly that that first marriage was an aggression by adults against a child and was wrong.

11. She was much more hesitant in telling of her marriage to Gregory, Christine's husband. She was reluctant to name him and spoke in a low voice. She looked down, embarrassed. Na´-

uwaGakh had been dead for some time whereas Gregory was very much alive and living in this village. Also, perhaps she was not so sure that she was justified in refusing him. While she and Nicholas seemed to get along well, still Gregory was more prosperous.

12. She had accepted her stepbrothers although she never had accepted her stepfather. She did not mention that her stepfather was married again for a year before his death.

13. Lydia must have been fifteen or sixteen years old when she married Nicholas.

NICHOLAS

Ernest Norton, Interpreter

Nicholas and I had not known each other previously. For this reason and because he was one of the first to tell me about his early life, I got only a short fragmentary account from him. Nicholas was a pleasant-appearing man, yet a man who seemed to keep himself apart and about whom I had heard almost nothing. He was approximately thirty-six years old at this time.

1. My family came from the mainland, from a large village east of Nelson Island. We came in a wooden sailing ship, a schooner. I was very small, maybe three years old or a little older. That was the first time I was on a boat like that and my first time on the sea. I can remember how the water sparkled—like crystals.

2. We came to Ka´nigiakhtuli´gamiut. I played with Gregory and didn't get homesick. When I was a boy, I played mostly with Gregory and Ki´oGan. The other children were friendly when I came, not hostile because I was a stranger.

[Gave list of families at that village.]

3. I had an older sister who married Aaron later. A brother died when he was little. My father and mother never separated.

4. These are things I especially remembered in my childhood: once I found a baby spotted seal on shore. I hit it with a stick and it wiggled into the water. When I told my parents, they scolded me a lot. I was little, I did not realize the value of a baby spotted seal.

5. I was frightened by the spirits in the Bladder Feast. It was a long time before I found out who they were.

6. My first kayak was made for me by my brother-in-law Aaron, a much older man, chief of the village. My father was living but

148

I was helped by Aaron. I was living with him. I learned hunting by myself; I did not go hunting with my father and I had no brothers.

7. When I was old enough to go hunting, I found a dead mukluk on shore and foxes feeding on it. I trapped two white foxes there. After that, I never was afraid to go hunting. I hunted regularly then.

8. The greatest fear I have known: one time when the men took a sweat bath at the beginning of the Bladder Feast, they made the kazigi too warm and spoiled the seal bladders. They took down the bladders, hung up seal stomachs instead. It was very serious. After a few years, we got seals again. The seals came back after a while. The village was very frightened.

9. Once I killed a female mukluk and her male pup with one shot! I found them together on shore. I don't get mukluk and walrus every year, but I usually get them.

10. Ka´nigiakhtuli´gamiut gave the Messenger Feast occasionally, and invited the whole island. Everyone in the village helped give it—no one man gave the feast.

11. In the village I came from [on the mainland], people did not have the Bladder Feast.

12. I married May; then I married Jessie (later she was married to Richard), and then Lydia. Lydia grew up in the same village I lived in. Now I'm married and have four kids. I don't do anything but work for them. I don't know anything more.

NOTES

1. Ernest said that Nicholas' own father had died on the mainland. Nicholas' mother remarried and his stepfather brought the family to Nunivak just to find a better place to live. He was not a Nunivak man.

2. I asked Nicholas how the other children treated him at first, when he was a stranger.

6. Nicholas' mother died and the man whom he and others always referred to as his father, TaLiˈlikh, probably was married to Rachel by this time. See Rachel's account.

7. Nicholas seems to have had difficulty in starting out to hunt on the sea.

8. Since Nicholas seemed to be a stable person, I asked him to describe the greatest fright he ever had had. Although I asked twice whether hunters caught any seals that year, he answered both times in the same way, avoiding the question regarding that particular year.

9. This must have been the greatest hunting achievement of his life.

10. He was asked to describe shaman performances that he had seen at these feasts. In answer, he gave these very meager general statements without any reference to shamans. I did not know at that time that Nicholas' stepfather, TaLiˈlikh, had been a much-feared shaman. Nicholas either did not know me well enough and trust me sufficiently to talk about shamans or else the subject was repugnant to him, which was not unlikely. He had been more or less estranged from his stepfather.

12. A young man who came in and heard the end of Nicholas' story told me later that Nick had talked to him about his marriage to May. Nick had loved her, but Aaron did not approve of her. One time when Nicholas returned from hunting, he found that Aaron had sent May home. Nicholas felt very bad, but he did not try to get May again. In the old days, most people felt that they had to submit to the wealthy men. Moreover, Nicholas evidently was dependent upon Aaron socially as well as materially.

SCANDAL

VIRGINIA CANNON

The two crucial events so far in Virginia's young life—she was nineteen years old in 1946—had occurred nearly fifteen years apart: in 1931 and 1945. Virginia and her half sister Emily, the latter adopted by Ernest and Rosamond Norton, were both big-boned, husky-looking girls. Virginia was the bad girl of the island at this time because in the early fall of 1945 she had become pregnant although she had no husband. Bernard Larson, her husband, had left her some time previously. The appearance of the baby confirmed community suspicions: while Virginia was not dark skinned, still the baby was unusually white skinned, obviously the child of a white man. In addition to the Reindeer Service men, about whom there was little or no suspicion, there had been the crew of the "Rocket," a Government motorship, and the crew of a small naval vessel that was anchored at Mekoryuk for a short while. (The name of the motorship has been changed.) Virginia was a Nash Harbor girl, but for a short while she had lived in Mekoryuk and done housework for the teachers.

She visited Mekoryuk only briefly while I was there, and I did not become well acquainted with her personally although I had known the story of her family for several years. In the following conversation, practically a monologue, Virginia used various devices to protect her reputation, and I did not deny them to her. This was not recorded in her exact wording, but is close enough to it, I think, so that I dare present it in the first person.

1. I'm married: I have a husband, but my husband left me. Emily is too young to marry yet. She's older than Dorothy, though: Dorothy got married when just a little girl. But Dorothy got a baby

in her before she was married. That's why she got married so young.

2. Charlie Sharp wants to marry Kate, but Kate won't marry him. Kate likes white men. Last summer Kate went to the "Rocket" and to the Navy boat to be with men. The "Rocket" came down from Unalakleet with a white man and two Eskimo boys, brothers. One of the brothers was a good worker; the other brother was very lazy. Kate liked him but he was mean to her. She liked him even though he's no good. He didn't treat her right.

3. Diana and I are good friends. [Diana was a half Eskimo girl from the mainland who had worked at the Reindeer Project.] Diana doesn't like Mekoryuk people because they gossiped about her, they said she stayed with men. She didn't do it, though. Mekoryuk people had no reason to say things about her, and she doesn't want to come back here.

4. Is your mother living? I have no mother. I have a father, at Seattle, Washington. He's been there a long time. He writes to me regularly. But I haven't had a letter from him for about a year.

5. I live with my aunt, Judy's mother, at Nash Harbor. My aunt takes care of me.

COMMENTS

Dick Lewis had worked at the Reindeer Project in Mekoryuk in the late summer of 1945. Being a young unmarried man, he had been in the group of young people that included Diana, Kate, and others. He said he knew Virginia had spent two or three nights on the "Rocket." Also, one night he rowed Virginia and Diana to the Navy power barge and they all went aboard. When he and Diana left, they asked Virginia to come with them. She wouldn't do it, she said she would stay a while. No one was forcing her to stay. Dick then brought Diana ashore.

The teacher said that Virginia had been a satisfactory worker, and they had got along well. When Virginia's pregnancy became known, the schoolboys teased and ridiculed her. The teacher told them not to judge Virginia too harshly, as all people have faults and make mistakes, and then they were nicer to her, at least when at the schoolhouse. However, Virginia's maternal grandmother's brother, Harmon, sternly returned Virginia to Nash Harbor and kept her there until the baby was three months old. Why Harmon, rather than Pearl and her husband, Dan Johnson, was caring for

Virginia, was not explained. When Harmon had come to fetch Virginia, she did not want to go with him. She told the teacher that Harmon's new wife did not like her and was mean to her. She wanted to live with her aunt, Pearl, who was like a mother to her. But she gave in to Harmon's authority and went to his home at Nash Harbor.

A young woman, Esther, was observed following her husband everywhere he went. I asked another young woman why Esther so constantly and obviously watched her husband. The reason: because Virginia was trying to get him. Virginia was not even in the village most of the time, but she evidently now was a sexual threat—more or less real—and a scapegoat.

Such attitudes did not arise from Virginia's own behavior alone. They went back to events in her family when she was three and a half or four years old, recounted to me by Nash Harbor people. (Virginia's parental family and their relatives all lived in Nash Harbor when she was young.) When she was in her fourth year (1931), in the early fall Solomon Cannon, his wife Hannah, his daughter Virginia, his infant son, and a young man, Jerome, were staying on the west side of the island: at Kaya´gayeli´gamiut and also at a camp near it. The men came back to Nash Harbor, bringing the children but without Virginia's mother. They said that she had died and been buried at Kaya´gayeli´gamiut.

The teacher at Nash Harbor became suspicious. First, Sol's wife had not been ill; second, Solomon disliked his wife and was having a love affair with his wife's sister Pearl. (According to island records, he married still another woman in November 1931. The villagers never mentioned this to me, however.) Without letting Sol and Jerome know what he was doing, the teacher sent two young men, his nephew who had come from St. Michael to visit him and Ernest Norton, younger brother of Jerome, to the village on the west side to investigate. When they dug up the fresh grave, they found only a parka stuffed with grass.

They reported this to the teacher, and when a coast guard cutter made its annual visit, he asked its captain to go to the camp where the Cannon family and Jerome had stayed as well as to the village where the grave was found. Ernest served as interpreter. Jerome told where the body was; coast guard men dug and found it. The body had been stuffed into a caved-in old house, between fallen rafters and the side-wall.

The coast guard made a coffin for the body and took it away. The cutter also took Solomon and Jerome to Nome, where they were tried and convicted a year later, each being sentenced to thirty years in the penitentiary.

Virginia's infant brother died soon after their mother was killed. Pearl kept Virginia and also had her own baby, Emily, Solomon's child born the preceding spring.

Nunivakers did not blame Jerome much. He was a serious-partner to Solomon and was obligated to help him, even to help him murder his wife. (A common version of the murder was that they had pushed her over a cliff.) Also, Jerome was younger than Solomon and undoubtedly was intimidated by him. In the penitentiary, Jerome became ill, evidently with tuberculosis. Although he was sent to a hospital, he died.

In the late 1930's, the trader on Nunivak received a letter—so he told Nunivakers—asking whether the people wanted Solomon to return, since he now could be paroled for good behavior. The more timid people would say nothing. Others said that they did not want him. He had been a bad man even before he killed his wife. He stole and did other things that Nunivakers did not like.

Solomon must have had subnormal intelligence or been an unusually maladjusted person—compared with normal Nunivak behavior—in order to murder his wife. In a society in which marital separation still was common and easy, certainly he did not have to murder her in order to get rid of her and marry Pearl. (Solomon's child Emily was not nearly so intelligent as Pearl's children by another man, but at this late date we cannot explain Emily's condition.) Possibly Sol had an uncontrolled sex drive. Everyone agreed that he was infatuated with Pearl. Virginia appeared to be sexually aggressive; and she had a kind of emotionality and lack of realism that were not unknown among Nunivakers but that were rare. Virginia appeared to have average intelligence. Her insecure, even traumatic, childhood in an atmosphere of community hostility to her father was sufficient to account for her difficulties of social conformity. Just as Solomon had been aggressive and irresponsible (unsocialized), perhaps even psychotic, as shown in theft, sexual relations, intimidation of a partner, and murder, so Virginia was aggressive in her speech and in sexual relations.

Because the Cannon case had been a very disturbing experience for Ernest Norton—I had reason to think that he had not yet recovered from its shock—I never mentioned it to him, but did have good opportunity one day to talk to him about Emily and Virginia. He discussed them with freedom and honesty, as follows:

Emily, his adopted daughter, was illegitimate, because Sol "went after Pearl for love" while still married to Hannah. Ben Martin (Uyuˀkochiˀakh), even though he was unmarried, had adopted Emily when she was very young. (Thus Pearl kept her niece, Virginia, and gave up her own child.) Then Ben married Rosamond and together they took care of Emily. Ben got typhoid fever (?) and was sent to the hospital at Kanakanak and died there. Ernest then married Rosamond and adopted Emily when she was five years old. She was not bright like her half brothers and half sister in the Cook family (said regretfully); on the other hand, she was not like her half sister, Virginia.

I asked how Virginia had acted when a little girl and how others had acted toward her.

Ernest said that when Pearl was taken to Nome as a witness at Solomon's trial, she took Virginia with her. After their return, Virginia told Ernest that Pearl had "talked hard" to her. Among other things, Pearl had told her that her (Virginia's) father was crazy. Yet Pearl thought she too should go "outside" and marry Solomon when he was sent out. (She of course had no conception of a penitentiary.) Virginia evidently had forgotten these things, said to her when she was only four or five years old, but Ernest remembered her telling him.

While Virginia was living at Nash Harbor, she was a good girl. She had always been well behaved until the preceding summer when she came to Mekoryuk. She spent nights on the Navy vessel, on the "Rocket" and with men on shore. (Ernest implied that she "went after" men.) She had told stories about Kate that were not true. Ernest was sure that Kate never had spent a night on any of the boats.

By tone and emphasis, he blamed Pearl more than Virginia, yet Virginia should not have behaved as she had; what she did was inexcusable. Virginia was not a good girl like Ernest's foster daughter, Emily.

Actually, Emily was watched closely, and it can be assumed that Virginia had been guarded at Nash Harbor all during adolescence. (It was said that Bernard had left her because she was "too young.") As a result, neither girl had had realistic experience in making choices and guiding herself. And both were starved for some means of expressing their emotions, as Emily showed in her projective tests.

Pearl must certainly have felt some guilt for having been the "cause" of Virginia's losing father, mother, and brother, and of her own sister's murder. (She gave the English name of her sister to the only child she bore after this.) So she kept Virginia and gave away her own child in infancy. Possibly she rejected, emotionally as well as physically, Emily, the evidence of her illegitimate relationship to Sol, who was "crazy" and a murderer. But Pearl, having been hurt, had to fight back and hurt someone else. Unfortunately, she took out her anger on Virginia, so that when the latter was grown, although Virginia regarded Pearl as a mother, she charged that "people" talked mean to her, attacked her. Virginia grew up knowing that her world was suspicious of her and ready to talk mean. Then, unfortunately, she gave it a good excuse.

NOTES

1. Virginia offered no explanation or excuse for Bernard leaving her. She was only establishing her married status so that she would not be labeled an unmarried mother.

Virginia said in effect that even Dorothy from a family of good reputation became pregnant when not married, and the father was the missionary's son.

2. She projected onto Kate, a young widow, her own behavior and attitudes. She probably was revealing here that, whoever was the father of her child, she was emotionally involved only with this Eskimo or part Eskimo boy.

3. Next, she identified with Diana who was innocent, so Virginia was innocent. Diana had left and did not want to return to Nunivak, so Virginia wanted to leave too?

4. Virginia's eyes filled with tears when she said that she had no mother and that her father was in Seattle.

5. She was referring to her maternal aunt, Pearl, who had reared her.

TEN YEARS LATER

Following are sequels which were collected during a visit to Nunivak Island of a few weeks in the winter of 1955-56.

DANIEL

Daniel died in January, 1951, probably of pneumonia. He was thought to be eighty years old. In January, 1956, his wife was still living and caring for two grandchildren. Two of their children had died, one of tuberculosis soon after Daniel told his story and one by drowning when out hunting. Three sons still lived on the island, supporting large families.

CHRISTINE GREGORY

At forty years, in December, 1950, Christine died of tuberculosis. Her eldest daughter died in a government hospital, also of tuberculosis and pneumonia. When Gregory married a younger woman who already had a family of her own, the two eldest sons of Christine and Gregory were angered. One son, especially, quarreled with his father. By the summer of 1956, the older son had attended boarding school, been hospitalized in a tuberculosis sanatorium in Washington State, been discharged, and enrolled in a high school there, where he was doing well. The second son, after working in a west Alaska trading center, was drafted for military duty.

Gregory and the teen-age daughter, who was not yet of school age when Christine told her story, were trying to maintain the home for the younger children while the second wife was in a tuberculosis hospital.

ZACHARY

In 1951, in his seventies, Zachary died, probably of tuberculosis. Thereafter, his wife lived with one of the poorer, unprogressive families. The new world, however, touched even the old lady: when she got sick in the winter of 1955-56, she was taken by plane to the government district hospital.

NU'SAN

When her husband retired from his mission, Nu'san accompanied him back to the mainland. One of her husband's daughters had married a Nunivak man and they also lived on the mainland where they could be easily visited. Even so, at her age she must have been homesick for Nunivak.

PAUL SCOTT

Both Paul and Anne were hospitalized for tuberculosis, in a large federal hospital, Paul a year longer than his wife. While in the hospital, he was strongly influenced by a fundamentalist religious sect. Not long after his discharge in 1956, he moved his family to the mainland, to be near his mother and his stepfather.

Although Melissa's grandfather had died, she still lived with her grandmother. Five sons and the stepson of Paul were still living in 1956 although one son had died in 1952 at one year of age and the three youngest boys had been taken by others, at least temporarily, during Anne's and Paul's illness. Both Thomas and Leila were treated for tuberculosis, in a different hospital from the one where their father and stepmother were sent; then after discharge, they were sent to a government boarding school for their high school education.

Paul had been a member of the Nunivak Council, advancing to its presidency the year before his hospitalization.

Paul's and Christine's families moved from a typical traditional life, through local leadership in a difficult acculturation period, on into the outside world where they probably will flounder a bit. Let us hope that that world will not be too hard for them.

RICHARD CHAPPEL

Less than a year after our 1946 sessions, Richard died of "blood poisoning." This ended not only an unhappy marriage and the final sad period of his life but also an entire family of shamans. Neither Richard nor his brothers left any known children.

EDWIN LARSON

Four years later, Edwin and his wife died in the same month, she apparently of injuries when she fell from a height onto the ice and he of pneumonia and perhaps also of shock.

The son married a daughter of Nicholas and Lydia and ten years later was living on the island; by now he was a village leader. He had one of the best frame houses, was a foreman at the Reindeer Project, secretary-treasurer of the council, assistant store manager, and weather and radio man. He had fulfilled and vindicated his father's aspirations.

LUTHER NORTON

Luther's wife died in 1953, thought to be in her seventies. Soon he married Ada, presenting her with a wolverine skin, following the old marriage custom which required that a parka or the skins for a parka be given the bride. He and especially his family continued in poor health, but he worked at his wood carving. He carved masks, wooden boxes and other items for sale, in those periods when the missionaries did not try to prevent the men making the masks. He lived a rather quiet life at Nash Harbor, a responsible but unassuming man.

RALPH JOHNSON

Ralph had had temper tantrums throughout childhood and even into adolescence. After he lost his fight with the council and suffered other frustrations, symptoms developed, reminiscent of the tantrums. He would have a "seizure," with trembling of the whole body, gasping breath, and staring eyes. This would occur when he was criticized or scolded, disappointed, or when in close proximity to Louise. He beat Rose and Louise and tried more than once to make love to Louise when she was in her early teens. (That Louise was a provocative girl trying to get attention was not mentioned locally.)

The council, prodded by the teacher, asked that Ralph be committed, and he was, in an old-style hearing by a United States Commissioner, without psychiatric examination. After two years in a stateside mental hospital, Ralph returned with a new skill: housepainting.

When he was seen at Mekoryuk in the winter of 1955-56, not long after his return, Ralph seemed emotionally flat, compared with the intensity of his earlier reactions. Louise, an attractive neurotic girl, was living at the teacherage and later was sent to boarding school. Ralph still humored Harriet, getting her special foods at considerable expense. He had had one mild seizure since his return, but he was a careful, methodical workman, and the prognosis appeared good so long as he had no serious provocation.

OLIVER

Compared with the great changes, the tragedies and excitements in some of the other families, Oliver's course was quiet. He and Agnes lost a two-year-old son, otherwise he and his family did well. He became a leader at Nash Harbor and was on the Nunivak Council for two years.

ETHAN

In January, 1956, Ethan and his wife had five living children. Since he told his story, one of their children had died in infancy, not an unusual occurrence in this area. He had moved into a responsible position in the community, elected to the Nunivak Council three successive years. He had not changed basically, however. He was known to have seen, in recent years, in one of the school classrooms—a substitute for the old kazigi—a "little man."

DICK LEWIS

Before long, Dick married a shy girl, daughter of a respected hunter. By 1956 he had three children and was a leader in community and Reindeer Project. He was not on the council, however, since his father was still an active leader and a member of the council.

He still was concerned about conformity to modern standards. He insisted on building a new-style frame house on piling, not banked with sods as other houses were, evidently for reasons of prestige.

FREDERICK MATTHEW

Fred went to Bethel, a trade-center, to work in a government installation. He married an acculturated mainland girl and had one child, a girl, before he was hospitalized for tuberculosis, in the same stateside hospital to which Christine's son was sent. There, he did well in craft work, but on his return home he went back to his former job, disregarding the old hunting and the new crafts. In 1957, he had a comfortable house, was accounted a good husband and father, and was leading a quiet life.

His older brother was still a hard-working leader on the island, held by a large and still growing brood of youngsters. To get money, he brought seal oil to trade on the mainland and occasionally worked in a mine. He evidently had the same drive as his father.

HELENE STEPHENS

During the next winter, Stephen died. Helene then married Adam Larson, a hard-working quiet widower with several children. Nine years after Stephen's death, Helene still had her adopted son and also five of Adam's own children and adopted children.

Her daughter, still quarreling with her husband but bearing children regularly, was unhappy and obese, and she had old-type visions, even in recent years. The son-in-law was disorganized, unable to take his family and village responsibilities; probably was mildly psychotic. Because of reports that he molested first old ladies, then young girls, the village disliked him.

Helene had not got away from her spirits entirely. Other people said that within recent years she had been taken by the Northern Lights and sent back unharmed, but they were not sure whether she had thereby acquired new power.

One cannot help thinking that shamanism channeled and expressed, in a locally acceptable way, her unhappiness and early hostility. Her sister Rachel, who presented a happier picture of childhood, must have been nevertheless a person full of a kind of hostility that drove people away from her. Helene, on the other hand, was rather attractive.

RACHEL, LYDIA, AND NICHOLAS

In 1947, Lydia died following childbirth, and the infant also died. Within the year, Nicholas married Rachel, at one time wife of his stepfather. Her son, Arthur, was the son of that stepfather. I never had learned whether, emotionally or in sense of family duty, Nicholas regarded Arthur as a half brother. Certainly he had not regarded Rachel as a mother. But had he been submissive to Lydia, therefore found it natural to marry another woman who tried to dominate people? Or did he marry her to get a housekeeper for his children?

In any case, he left her (she died of influenza in 1953) and in 1951 took his children, Norbert and Ella, to a mainland village, where he lived with a woman who was a stranger to Nunivakers. He committed suicide and his mistress soon abandoned the children. They were taken from one mainland village to another by people whose motives and relationship to the children were not clear. Finally, their older sister Lottie, wife of Joe Larson, heard of the children's bad state. Ella had disappeared but Norbert finally was brought back to Nunivak and adopted by the Larsons.

VIRGINIA CANNON

Virginia was assisted before long in taking her baby away from Nunivak, to southeast Alaska, in order to give it hospital care. She got a job and slowly began making a new life.

She went to one of the larger towns to work, married, and settled down. From 1955 to 1957 at least, she was known to be living in an urban locality, apparently married happily.

In 1949, Solomon Cannon returned to Nunivak from the penitentiary where he had served about seventeen years. He spoke English, had gained weight, was of course middle-aged, and was received as a kind of strange resurrection.

He had been paroled to the missionary who, knowing the requirements of local life, permitted Sol to have a gun for hunting, regardless of the parole regulations, and later permitted him to marry.

About 1952, when out hunting alone, he killed an animal that he thought was a fox. When he came up to it, he discovered that it was a wolf, shot at such great distance that it looked small like a fox. This feat, settling a big argument as to whether there really was a wolf killing the reindeer, and ending the depredation, re-established Sol in the community. Symbolically, he reverted from English to Eskimo speech.

CONCLUSION

These accounts revealed inadvertently much that had not previously been told. The following behavior and attitudes appeared often
enough so that one can make some new generalizations regarding
the functioning of Nunivak culture.

1. Young people in their first marriage, when still boys and
girls, were likely to be unhappy. These arranged marriages did
not work so well as the elders had led me to believe. The successive marriages are easier to understand when one sees how difficult it was for youngsters to accept marriage. One sees also at
least some of the circumstances and sequels of plural marriages,
which might or might not be happy, just as with single marriages.

2. The effect on children of the old-time brittle marriage is
especially graphic. Sometimes, because of a parent's death, break-
up of a family was unavoidable, but also sometimes the family
broke up because of apparently immature emotional needs of a
parent, with very little consideration for the needs of the child.
Although there were customs of kindness and tolerance toward children, the society centered in the adult males. The good hunter or
shaman could take or discard women and children as he wished,
short of physically mistreating them.

3. The handing of a child around from one family to another might
bring him or her into better circumstances, economically and emotionally, or into worse. Perhaps, with kinsmen's intervention,
the child would not be allowed to languish so long in a bad situation
as can happen in our more complex society, yet individual children
seem to have suffered from a broken family and adoption just as
much as in societies not so noted for permissiveness and kindness
to children. In fact, the Eskimo reputation in this regard probably
is exaggerated.

It may have been, of course, that because most children were

well treated by their parents, they were especially hurt and resentful when given to someone else.

Because adoption was so common in Eskimo society, there was
a great chance that any one Eskimo child would have the variable
experience of adoption. Yet here as elsewhere individuals differed in economic success and generosity. It is all the more important, then, to see this variation. The usual ethnographic account of customs and social forms reveals neither individual advan-
tage nor damage. Case material is a necessary supplement.

4. From this material it appears that village leaders not uncom-
monly were petty tyrants. They might be admired, envied, disliked
by other men, depending on the position and needs of those others.
There seem to have been inadequate checks on antisocial behavior.
Song satires had disappeared, if indeed they ever had existed here.
The chief recourse of a misused person was flight from his family
or community. In reaction to a disliked leader, a whole group of
people would move out of his kazigi or his village.

There was gratitude for good leaders, too, explicitly stated
occasionally although this did not make so interesting a subject
for anecdotes as did wife stealing, or quarrels between top hunters,
or sorcery.

5. Submissiveness of young adults toward their elders is abun-
dantly illustrated in these autobiographies. Yet we see that they
had ways of quietly rebelling, too. Again, a common reaction was
flight. Thus aggression was avoided, yet one's attitude was made
plain.

It is fruitless to talk of bravery, cowardice, timidity: these
words imply values that may be inappropriate to Nunivak culture.
Nunivakers can be said, with fair scientific objectivity, to be realistic regarding their world, physical and social. The price of lack
of realism, lack of caution, was high: it was likely to be death,
or a lifetime of ostracism or fear.

6. Although the sample is small, our two cases of shamans agree
well in showing lonely children who felt rejected, who thus were
powerfully motivated to escape into a dream existence, but who
also were deliberately taught shamanism. Both said, moreover,
that they were urged on by the community. (This may have been
self-justification.) They agreed, too, in saying that at first they
were frightened by spirits, then reached a point at which they lost
fear and gained mastery over the spirits, at least sufficiently to
travel in the spiritual realm without being lost. This escape from
reality brought a tranquilizing peace to Richard, but only fitful
peace and satisfaction to Helene. Being a more aggressive person,

she had more guilt to contend with. Richard could feel himself the innocent victim of hostility. Helene, on the other hand, met opposition with equal hostility. He was submissive; she was dominating.

There is an intriguing hint of another shared trait: latent, not overt, homosexuality. Richard's fear of falling into a crack, of being engulfed, and several other symbols in his visions, his favorite myths, and his Rorschach test suggest at least concern regarding potency and fear of heterosexual relations, if not specifically homosexuality. In Helene's case, the evidence centers in her relationship to her daughter. The village regarded her possessive love for her daughter as excessive. The dynamics of her parental family, that is, the kind of relationship among its members, were propitious for development of this trait. It might be suggested that Helene simply was a compulsive loving mother because her own mother had not been, in her view; but this would not be incompatible with a homosexual tendency or at least conflict regarding relations with the opposite sex. I do not suggest, by any means, that this is an essential or important trait in a shaman's personality. It may have been true, though, that for most shamans their sex relations were accompanied by anxiety, just as their other relationships were disturbed and anxiety-ridden.

7. There was considerable individual difference in acceptance of the old religion, and not all of it can be explained by acculturation and the differences between older and younger generation. Even in the category of middle-aged people, there were unexpected differences in belief in amulets and especially in accepting the Bladder Feast spirits. In the traumatic situation of being given to the spirits, supposedly to be eaten, some Eskimo children kept their wits sufficiently to observe and explain the details rationally. Others accepted what they were told.

8. Suspicion of all Caucasians and hostility toward some were more evident in this material than in interviews and other kinds of data. They were no stronger than individual Nunivakers' feelings against other individual Nunivakers, but they seemed to be more general in the adult population. In view of the damage suffered at the hands of whites, not nearly all of which was told in the autobiographies, the Nunivak people remained remarkably realistic and discriminating, differentiating between "good" and "bad" individual Caucasians.

9. Acculturation differences between young and old do appear although it is hard to make a comprehensive assessment from this kind of material. The young people were more willing to talk to

an outsider about both personal relations and the old culture. Oliver, for example, was willing to identify his "real" totemic animal spirit-helper. Possibly the young people simply had not yet been hurt so much as their elders and had not grown cautious. It is just as possible that they no longer feared the sanctions enforcing secrecy of certain parts of the ancient religion.

10. The old culture appears less heroic when one sees it in actual cases rather than in generalization. The boy's first seal catch might not be harpooned out among the ice floes but might easily be a seal pup caught on shore. The young hunter required to fast during the Bladder Festival recalls this not as a spiritual experience but as an occasion when he had a headache and felt bad. Yet offsetting such loss of glamour in the Eskimo way of life, there is an increase of real tragedy and of the strength in adversity that most individuals have shown. Individualism is maintained along with voluntary submission to the demands of the community and the accidents of fate.

True, this was the behavior of most people; but among our subjects, in later years one had a mental break, one committed suicide (immediate cause unknown), while two not among our subjects committed suicide in hospitals and at least one other person appeared psychotic. In a population not exceeding two hundred, the total of these cases presents a disturbing figure, from a humanitarian standpoint. In regard to culture generalization, it confirms satisfactorily the statement that Nunivakers must conform and submit or take flight: physically, perhaps by leaving the island, or psychologically, in psychotic behavior or religious fantasy life. Two men became sexually aggressive, but no one became overtly antisocial in other ways. (Modern Eskimo leaders as a group are less selfish, more responsible socially than their predecessors. It may be that the white leaders have taken the place of the old-time "boss of the kazigi" or the shaman who made his own rules for social behavior!) The biggest question for this Eskimo group is not "how does the community handle the individual's aggression?" but "how does the individual handle his own aggression?"

With the exception of the above increase in realism in our portrayal of Nunivak culture, meaning chiefly an increase in variation of behavior, no great changes need be made in the ethnography as a result of the autobiographies and their sequels. The material circumstances and the basic values of Nunivak were as seen previously. What we have added is depth (the depth of effect on the person by material and social requirements), and variation in meaning and response. The subjective side of culture, especially a subjective view of shamanism, has been turned toward us for the first time in this locality. We are grateful to the Nunivak people for their willingness to reveal their experiences and their emotions.

APPENDIXES

APPENDIX A. RORSCHACH TESTS

The Rorschach raters were Dr. Eugenia Hanfmann, clinical psychologist, and Dr. Alice Joseph, psychiatrist. In 1949, when the interpretations were made, both were employed at the Harvard Psychological Clinic. The author is grateful to both for their excellent cooperation in a difficult experiment.

Of the thirty-two subjects tested in 1946, eight also gave their autobiographies. Only these eight are presented here.

To reduce length and to make the interpretations easier to read, the original rating sheets are not reproduced here; instead, the raters' entries on them and their explanatory notes are combined. We give first the traits on which they agreed, then the ones on which they disagreed. On some, a little comment by the author is added, but interpretation of the life history (or portion of it obtained) and test in relation to each other is largely left to the reader. Each person can use these materials according to his own interest.

For a more detailed explanation of the Rorschach rating project, see Lantis, 1953, pp. 140-45.

CHRISTINE GREGORY

Dr. Hanfmann and Dr. Joseph agreed that Christine was more extrovert than introvert, with affection directed to many rather than few, but disagreed on the strength of her affection for others and on ease of changing objects of affection. Hanfmann: "Her careful and secure adaptation to environment probably enables her to get along with different people."

They agreed that anxiety was low. Regarding defenses against anxiety, Hanfmann suggested "channelizing of her energies into activities which serve avoidance of emotional areas, and are also satisfying in themselves. "

One interpreter of the test tended to state her view on the subject more forcefully than the other and saw certain traits or problems of the subject as more intense. Sex conflict: "much." Aggression: "high." Inhibition of aggressive impulses: "marked." The other scorer said, "little," "slight," and "moderate" on these three. They agreed that repression and suppression were noticeable defenses against aggressive expression.

The raters agreed that the subject did not have strong feelings of guilt, that she was, in general, conforming and had only moderate or slight fear of or reaction against coercion. Hanfmann: "She appears neither very fearful nor very rebellious. "

' Joseph thought the test showed marked dependency strivings, Hanfmann thought they were slight, adding, "appears too active to be very dependent." (They may have been thinking of different levels of such striving in the subconscious.) Similarly, regarding wish to dominate, Hanfmann rated this "slight." Joseph rated it "marked, but ambivalent," as one would expect if both dependency striving and wish to dominate are high.

They agreed that Christine had superior intelligence and was very persistent, that the quality of intelligence was practical rather than abstract or imaginative. Joseph also saw high energy output. Despite the subject's abilities, Joseph thought there still existed, because of her persistence, wish to dominate, etc., a considerable gap between her achievement strivings and abilities. Hanfmann, in line with her other ratings, thought the achievement strivings not unrealistic.

The interpreters saw little evidence of pathology except that the subject might be obsessive-compulsive, to which Joseph added the possibility of psychosomatic symptoms and rigidity, while Hanfmann added possible mood-swings. The latter was more hopeful about Christine's adjustment: "She had considerable assets, and her anxieties seem to be well taken care of. " The very fact that Drs. Joseph and Hanfmann disagreed regarding the nature of Christine's problems—one said they arose from concerns of "physical competence," the other said "internal conflicts"—suggests that the problems either were small or were hidden without too much discomfort.

LUTHER NORTON

Drs. Hanfmann and Joseph agreed regarding Luther:

Affection: Moderate to strong, directed toward many people rather than a few. (On the question as to whether he could easily change objects of affection, they disagreed.)

Sex conflict: Little or none.

Defense against own aggressive impulses: Projection. To this might be added "escape into reality" and repression.

Conscious anxiety: Moderate or low. Hanfmann: "Though his constriction may indicate anxiety, it also probably takes care of it. May have slight depressive trends. "

Sources of anxiety: The nonhuman world, the world in general. Joseph added "people, " Hanfmann added "incompetence. "

Feeling of guilt: Moderate or slight, i. e. , neither markedly high nor low. (But regarding shame, they disagreed.)

Conformity-individuality: A conforming person.

Dependency: Yes. The raters differed a little regarding degree of dependency.

Reaction to domination: No fear; fairly easily dominated.

Wish to dominate: Little or none.

Miscellaneous needs and drives: Striving for a general security. One rater added desire for material goods, competition, and jealousy.

Energy output: Moderate.

Persistence: High.

Intelligence: High average.

Quality of thinking: Practical.

Striving for achievement: Some discrepancy between abilities and striving, but not a marked difference.

Rigidity-flexibility in thinking: Rigid.

Clinical pathology: No. But both raters noted the subject's rigidity as a pathological tendency, to which one added "suspicion. "

Adjustment: Fairly good. Hanfmann: "Seems well adjusted in a stereotyped impersonal fashion. "

Source of adjustment problems: Internal conflict. Joseph: "Constriction suggests character disturbance. "

Elements of Luther's personality that the raters could not agree on so well were:

Extroversion-introversion: More extroverted or midway on this scale.

Blocking of either: General blocking or only of extroversive expression.

Aggression: Moderate or slight.

Inhibition of aggression: Marked or moderate.

Shame: None or a moderate amount of shame.

The questions are understandable regarding a person who is conforming, constricted and dependent. Extroversion, aggression, and expression of shame would not have much opportunity to show clearly. A person who is timid when dealing with strange or strong people or in a strange physical situation is at a considerable disadvantage when taking a test. Any counteracting forces in him may have difficulty showing up. It is to the credit of the test and the raters that Luther was described so well.

RALPH JOHNSON

The raters agreed on this subject well beyond expectation. (They should not be expected to agree on exact degree of all traits. On a Rorschach Test, some kinds of personality traits apparently are more easily evaluated than others. Also, the interpreters express their ideas with different degrees of force or certainty, according to their own personality or according to situation.)

They agreed that his tendency is toward extroversion more than introversion but that he is blocked in expressing his extroversion.

His tendency to affectionate relationships is "moderately strong" or "weak: this may be underestimating it, but in the total picture of conflict this aspect is lost." He can change the object of affection. However, whether affection is directed to few or many people was not agreed on.

He is highly aggressive but overt aggression is markedly inhibited. His principal defense mechanism is repression, to which Joseph added "evasion" and Hanfmann added "suppression" and "possible symptom-formation."

His anxiety is high, the principal source of the subject's anxiety being his feeling of incompetence; but relations with people cause him some anxiety, too. Joseph added that the natural world also seems threatening to him. Both interpreters, in answer to the question regarding subject's defenses against anxiety, wrote in: "avoidance."

He has little individuality.

His striving for a dependency role was rated "moderate" and "slight: such strivings would be interfered with by the conflict about aggression."

He has marked fear of being dominated by others; he wants autonomy. This was less equivocal than the preceding. On the other hand, his own wish to dominate, like his need for dependency, is complicated. Joseph said his wish to dominate is marked. Hanfmann said, "He may wish to dominate, as protection against others, but doubt if he shows or pursues it (except by negativism)."

He has high-average intelligence but little energy output and only moderate or slight persistence. Intellectually, he is highly rigid; and there is a marked gap between his abilities and his goals. (That is, he wants to achieve much more than he is achieving or is capable of achieving. This agrees with his feeling of inadequacy.)

They agreed that there is evidence of mental pathology. Joseph: "Anxiety state with depressive and hypochondriacal features." Hanfmann: "Neurotic disturbance. High level of anxiety interfering with performance." "He comes closer than others so far seen to the neurotic picture familiar to us." Adjustment: poor or very poor. Source of adjustment problem: an internal conflict (rather than conflict with other people).

When the test interpreters tried to describe symptoms of the neurosis, they did not agree so exactly. One said Ralph is obsessive-compulsive, rigid, and hysteric. The other said he is withdrawn and hypochondriac. (These are not incompatible. Especially "hysteric" and "hypochondriacal" are general and specific aspects of the same behavior.)

Regarding a few miscellaneous needs and anxieties, the record is not so clear. One rater said Ralph seems much concerned about his security in interpersonal relations and possibly is jealous; the other has suggested competition rather than jealousy and also fear of physical danger, that is, a need to feel physically secure.

On two points, the ratings are rather surprising. (1) Neither interpreter rated sex conflict as high. One said, "None." The other said, "Some." (2) On shame or guilt, one said there is moderate guilt. The other said guilt is marked, "in the form of feelings of incompetence." In other words, she apparently did not see much other evidence of guilt.

The community has treated Ralph as inferior, surely strengthening whatever feelings of inferiority he had from psychological sources. Whether the community's behavior developed because of his illegitimacy or his periodic outbursts of aggression when his inhibition and rigidity were shattered, even in boyhood, it probably is now too late to decide. Perhaps the community merely supplied the form in which his basic conflict and guilt regarding the conflict could be expressed without punishment.

The hypochondria that one of the raters saw in Ralph's test seems to have been expressed, in life, in his excessive concern regarding his daughter's health and well-being, rather than concern for his own health. The whole question of his relationship to daughters and stepdaughter and stepson is intriguing. Perhaps his wish to dominate people has been directed neurotically toward children, not adults. Perhaps, since his extroversion and affection were blocked, dramatically in the loss of wife and two little girls or even earlier but less dramatically in some childhood situation, he now is obsessive-compulsive in expressing love for children.

Regarding Ralph's attempt to deal with his problems by avoidance and evasion, the modern culture helped. It gave him the opportunity to identify with Caucasians and try to live like them, to flee at least partially a situation in which he was treated with something close to contempt. Thus, as appears in his Rorschach protocol, he set a high goal and made some progress toward it. (It was helped later by his experience in the mental hospital, but the gap still is great.) However, such effort does not solve the basic problem.

ETHAN

Some of the personality characteristics of this man were so strong or well marked that there was no question about them. On others, there was a question of degree: was this trait or impulse "moderate" or "slight," "moderate" or "strong"? We shall look first at the items on which there was agreement.

Extroversion-introversion: Extroverted, even "very," with no blocking of expression of subject's extroversion (but there was some blocking of introversion). "Vivid impulsive response, though possibly with some conflict."

Sex conflict: Yes, some.

Anxiety: High; of a diffuse type. Also a focused anxiety, according to Joseph. Hanfmann: "may have depressive trends...or some introspective inclination."

Source of anxiety: People (stated strongly). Joseph added "incompetence" as a source of anxiety.

Fear of physical coercion: Marked.

Conformity-individuality: Not much individuality, i.e., generally conforming.

Wish to dominate: Marked.

Intelligence: Superior.

Quality of thinking: Imaginative.

Achievement strivings in relation to abilities: Only slight gap,
   i. e. , not unrealistic.
Rigidity-flexibility: Flexible.
Clinical pathology: No; but is impulsive. Hanfmann added that he
   possibly has mood-swings, homosexual tendencies, and a fantasy life. Joseph added feelings of organic inferiority and obses-
   sive traits. (These are not incompatible.)
Adjustment: Fairly good. Joseph added: "Good control. No serious
   breaks. "
   On the following traits, there was a difference of opinion, although in most cases not a strong difference.

	Rater No. 1	*Rater No. 2*
Affection	Moderate	Strong
Ability to change objects of affection	Easy. "May have a fear of permanent ties?"	Difficult
Aggression	Moderate	High
Inhibition of aggression	Slight	Moderate
Defenses against own aggression	"Has some stabilizing inner resources in his intelligence and imagination."	Projection. Escape into reality
Guilt and shame	No conclusion	Moderate
Striving for dependency	No conclusion	Marked
Fear of domination	Moderate	Marked
Miscellaneous traits	Possibly anxiety regarding achieving security (in general) and autonomy	Anxiety regarding security in interpersonal relations, avoidance of physical danger. Desire for material goods
Source of problems of adjustment	Internal conflicts and difficulties with people	Own physical competence

The fact that both raters noted this man's impulsiveness, intelligence and imagination, anxiety regarding his relations with people, and the other elements of his personality that appeared clearly in the test, convinces us that here is a consistent delineation of a man who finds expression in culturally approved fantasy. He would have seemed more aberrant in a culture not permitting religious visions.

Even the characteristics mentioned incidentally or mentioned by only one rater fit the delineation and also the realities of Ethan's life, for example his concern regarding his own competence, his fear of physical danger, his use of projection as a defense. (The one trait that does not fit is "escape into reality.") Along with these, we see his wish to dominate and fear of being dominated, even physically coerced, by others. Probably such a man is fortunate if he can escape, at least temporarily, into a fantasy world, especially a socially approved one.

The defense that Ethan so conveniently acted out, so that we do not have to suppose it, viz., repression, evidently did not show up in the Rorschach: neither rater even guessed at it.

RICHARD CHAPPEL

The interpreters of the test agreed well on this subject:
Introversion-extroversion: More extroverted, with some blocking of both.
Affection: Moderate.
Sex conflict: High.
Anxiety: High.
Sources of anxiety: Relations with people and own incompetence, to which Hanfmann added the nonhuman external world.
Feeling of guilt: None or slight, at least for conscious guilt.
Conformity-individuality: Little individuality.
Adjustment: Poor.
Source of adjustment problems: Difficulties with other people. Hanfmann added "physical competence."
Energy: Moderate or slight, i. e. , neither especially high nor low.
Persistence: Moderate or slight.
Pathology: No (Joseph); possibly (Hanfmann).
Nature of pathological trends or symptoms: Suspicion. One rater added that the subject perhaps was hysteric, impulsive, and had homosexual tendencies or was impotent.
Differences in interpretation were as follows:
Aggressiveness and inhibition of aggressive impulses: Aggression

high, with moderate inhibition; and aggression moderate, with marked inhibition. (The significance of this, probably, is that degree of aggression was not clearly evident.)
Intelligence: High average; low average.

As this was a rather poor, meager record, it is not surprising that Hanfmann did not try to evaluate it regarding certain areas of the personality and Joseph's evaluation was tentative. A few items, therefore, have been skipped.

Some of the myths that Richard told clearly contain sex symbolism, with indications of homosexuality. This interpretation of the myths was made before the interpretation of his Rorschach test was known. See Himmelheber, 1951, pp. 31-5, 55-61, 71-84, 92, 103-9; Lantis, 1946, pp. 298-300, and 1953, pp. 110-11, regarding the man named Kangalix or Gangelich.

HELENE

The raters agreed on the following items:
Subject has little or no sex conflict. One, however, added "frustrated sexual desires?"
Is highly aggressive. Hanfmann added, "Aggression to men . . . possibly others. "
Subject's principal defense is suppression. Joseph added projection and escape into activity. Hanfmann added repression, avoidance and evasion.
Has slight or no dependency strivings.
Has marked wish to dominate.
Is highly competitive.
Is very jealous.
Is concerned with achieving security in interpersonal relations. (Emphasis is on the concern, the anxiety, rather than achievement.)
Source of her adjustment problems is "people" rather than "internal conflicts" or "physical competence. "
Has no "need achievement, " that is, there is no gap between what she would like to accomplish and her abilities. (This fits the personality delineation since it refers to intelligence, physical ability, and success in practical affairs. It does not fit the poor accomplishment in personal relations.)
Is neither especially flexible nor rigid.
Has no pathology; but Joseph added, "Some suspicion of paranoid trends. . . . " Hanfmann added, "although the possibility of hys-

terical symptoms or some somatic involvement not excluded."
Adjustment not good. One rater said "fair," the other said "poor."
On the following items there was less agreement:

	Rater No. 1	*Rater No. 2*
Introversion-extroversion	More intro-verted	Ambiequal
Blocking of these tend-encies	None	Yes, both
Tendency to affection-ate relationships	Strong	Weak
Inhibition of aggression	Slight	Moderate
Level of conscious anxiety	Low, focused on males	Moderate, diffuse
Shame	None	Moderate
Guilt	None	Moderate
Fear of coercion	None	Moderate
Conformity and indi-viduality	Marked indi-viduality	Generally conforming but "content suggests she might have a quarrelsome, critical streak"
Fear of domination	None	Marked
Energy	High	Moderate
Persistence	High	Slight
Intelligence	Superior	No conclusion
Quality of intelligence	*Imaginative,* also practical and abstract	*Practical* but with po-tentialities for imagin-ative and abstract thinking
Pathological symptoms	Impulsiveness "in sense of following 'in-ner prompt-ings.'" Suspi-cion	Possibly obsessive compulsive and hys-teric

Despite the above differences, there appears clearly a picture of a woman who wants to get along with people but who, because of need to dominate, competitiveness, suspicion and jealousy, cannot do so and has anxieties, both conscious and unconscious, regarding her relations with people. We see that this is compatible with her life history. She could have an affectionate relationship only with those people, for example, her daughter and grandson, whom she could dominate. Hers was an essentially tragic life, somewhat relieved by her shamanism: subjectively, by the escape from reality that it provided; objectively, by its accomplishments for community good.

The seeming discrepancy between Rorschach interpretation and evidence from life history that is most interesting pertains to shame and guilt. At first it appears surprising that one or both of these did not show up markedly. It may have been that the Rorschach test did not tap these fully, or it may have been that in her autobiography Helene professed a shame that she did not feel. She may have been so resentful against mistreatment in childhood that all her subsequent behavior was justified. Actually, the rating of "moderate" shame and guilt is a good fit. Helene was not racked by guilt or shame but they were present, as she said.

NICHOLAS

This man's test evidently was difficult for the raters to interpret: it seemed hard for them to see him as a total personality. One of them left several blanks on the checklist. Nevertheless, they did agree on the following:

Nicholas was extroverted, with no blocking of his extroversion, and he sought warm affectionate relationships, not limiting such relationships to only a few people. One rater noted, "Emotionality vivid and seems to lack aggressive connotation." One thought he probably could change objects of affection ("not too rigid"), while the other suspected this might be hard for him, explaining that there was a suggestion of "latent introversial tendencies."

He seemed to have little or no sex conflict (neither rater felt sure on this question). Dr. Hanfmann explained: "Nothing shows, either little conflict or very well repressed."

There was some but not great inhibition of aggression. (See below for further discussion of aggression.)

Regarding kinds of defenses against his own aggressive impulses, "avoidance" and "denial" were mentioned with the explanation: "Somewhat vague perceptions and generalizations: might indicate *denial* of threatening situations. Would be in line with some childish features of the record." One rater suggested also "repression," and "projection." She mentioned "avoidance" again in regard to defense against anxiety.

Nicholas had low anxiety, at least "low 'conscious' anxiety," and little or no guilt or shame.

His fear of physical coercion and fear of being dominated were moderate. His striving for a dependence role was moderate. That is, he was neither especially high nor low in these personality dynamics. Similarly, he was conforming in most things, without much individuality.

He was acquisitive, to which Dr. Joseph added that he was competitive and possibly jealous.

He had high-average intelligence and moderate persistence. There was some gap—not a great one—between his striving for achievement and his abilities. He was neither unusually rigid nor flexible in his intellectual approach: he was "between."

There was no mental pathology. The one trait of possible significance for pathology that both interpreters mentioned was "impulsive." Hanfmann added "possible mood-swings," while Joseph added "hysteric," "feels organic inferiority."

To one rater, Nicholas appeared well adjusted, but the other expressed some doubt: "Too competitive for being well adjusted, but cautious front helps to convey impression of better adjustment."

Regarding differences of interpretation, one must note that three or four of the five traits on which the raters disagreed are probably related parts of a complex. Dr. Joseph thought aggression high in this man, that he had a marked wish to dominate, that his anxiety was focused on a specific problem—his relations with people—instead of being a diffuse feeling-tone, and that he had high energy-output. Dr. Hanfmann did not rate Nicholas as just the opposite, but did record questions and doubts on each of these points.

A final trait, on which clear difference was recorded, pertained to the quality of the subject's thinking. One rater said that it was "abstract" and to a lesser extent "imaginative," the other said "practical."

Dr. Hanfmann struggled to assess the relative importance of what she saw. She mentioned the "unaggressive character of the record," "medium output, easy responses, 'impressionistic' wholes," pointing out that these "might indicate susceptibility to coercion, as well as certain passivity" and "slight energy," but also might indicate that he would respond emotionally, that "in 'nonmental' matters his outgoingness may count for more."

In summary, there appears an outgoing, impulsive man, with moderate fears, little or no feeling of guilt or shame, no great individuality, and a willingness to conform in most situations. He was intelligent enough, not too rigid, but only moderately persistent and striving (for achievement). He had no strong conflicts although one rater suspected a problem regarding aggression and wish to dominate. No matter what lay underneath, externally he appeared well adjusted.

Later events suggest that the adjustment depended on marriage to a woman who was capable but not aggressive and self-centered. Nicholas evidently lacked within himself the strength to control his emotionality and impulsiveness. What transpired in the years after he gave his autobiography is compatible with the Rorschach interpretation, in fact is enlightened by the test.

VIRGINIA CANNON

According to her Rorschach Test, Virginia did not have much conflict regarding sex. There also was not much evidence of aggression, and not because aggression was inhibited: she did not seem to be strongly inhibited, the raters agreed. Her principal defense against her own aggression was repression, according to Dr. Joseph; Dr. Hanfmann said, "There is some prettifying and making harmless of emotions. . . ."
The subject showed moderate anxiety, both diffuse and focused, principal source of her anxiety being her feeling of incompetence. One rater added that the world in general might seem threatening to her, but "probably relations with people are not felt as very disturbing." Virginia's defense against anxiety was, according to Joseph, repression or, according to Hanfmann, "There might be flight into reality . . . and into cheerfulness."
Then Dr. Hanfmann recorded that she suspected moderate to marked guilt feelings, "suggested by tendency to depression, some self criticism. . . ." (Dr. Joseph thought there was not guilt but moderate shame.) As one would expect, Hanfmann said that the test indicated mood-swings in the subject.
She showed some wish to dominate and some competitiveness. Her persistence was slight or moderate, not high, and energy moderate or possibly high, "but if so, only in spurts, more vitality than *sustained* energy."
Virginia had high-average intelligence, of a practical type, with strong achievement strivings. (One rater thought her rigid in her

thinking, the other rated her neither markedly rigid nor flexible.)

They agreed that although she showed the following traits, they were not of clinically significant degree, that is, there was no clinically manifest pathology: *hysteric,* also *impulsive* although basically rigid, or showing mood-swings. She was very extroverted, without any blocking of expression of her extroversion (there was blocking of introversion) but how strong her real affection was, whether it was directed widely or onto only a few people and whether she could change objects of affection were not, evidently, so clear. (The raters disagreed on these.)

There was agreement that Virginia was fairly well adjusted, but "might break down on occasions. " The principal source of her adjustment problems was internal conflict. Dr. Hanfmann concluded, "Relations to people seem on the whole positive and controlled—[there is a] will to adjustment, " yet one must suspect "impulsivity and disturbance. "

APPENDIX B. GENEALOGIES*

  I. Families of Aaron, Nicholas, Lydia, and Elizabeth
 II. Families of PugulaGa´Lagia, Dennis, Ethan and Pani´-
     khkakh, and Edwin Larson
III. Families of Christine and Paul, Harmon, and Apa´zu
 IV. Families of Asael Sharp, Chu´qa, Russell, and Kapu´Gan
  V. Families of Daniel and Amelia, Kiawi´Gakh and A´naGaN,
     Stephen and Helene
 VI. Families of Larson, John, and Clarence
VII. Families of Herbert and Lucinda, Tim and Juliet, Ezra
     and Rose
VIII. Families of Tachi´Lka and ANa´Gakh, Ka´naga´Gan, and
     Wilson
 IX. Families of Simon, Lukhtusi´Gakh, Kusa´uyakh, Ernest
     Norton, Cook, and Solomon
  X. Families of Lewis, Benson, Pani´gaGakh, James, Chani´-
     aGaLagia, and A´qoaq

Note on Genealogies

Names of many of the young children, of the latest recorded generation, necessarily have been left blank. They are called usually
by their English names, which are obtained easily from school and
church records but which are not given here, to protect the children. Getting their Eskimo names is much more difficult, since
these can be obtained only from their Eskimo elders and best by

---

*All English names are fictitious.

189

interview: the Nunivakers' English spelling of their names is not exactly consistent or even recognizable. Unless these youngsters have been mentioned in the biographies, they have not been assigned fictitious English names. All English names shown in the genealogies are of course the fictitious ones.

These genealogies, obtained and checked on three visits to the island during sixteen years, should be considered current as of January, 1956; that is, no births and deaths since that time have been included. The basic work on the genealogies was done in 1939-40 when the author's field studies were supported by the American Philosophical Society, Philadelphia, and the Department of Anthropology, University of California, Berkeley.

The "mainland" from which some Nunivakers obtained spouses includes Nelson Island, since it is and has been socially part of the mainland. Geographically, the strait separating it from the mainland is no greater barrier than a small river. Nunivak, in contrast, was isolated by a twenty-three-mile-wide strait that was dangerous in all but the calmest weather and impassable in winter. Since 1940, however, with increasing air travel Nunivak has been increasingly accessible. The principal result thus far has been a drawing of Nunivakers to the mainland to live, reversing the trend in the early part of the century.

Notes on Relationships

I. The Cha´qa (135A) who was Helene's aunt may have been the Cha´qa who was the elder Scott's mother. If so, she would have been married (probably first) to A´pa´Gayakh and (second) to Kiogoyu´-Gakh. She is here treated as the same person, with a question mark.

The ANa´sakh (71A) whom Rachel married may have been the same man as Ezra's father (188A) who customarily was referred to by his nickname, ANa´sakh.

II. There is some evidence that the Larsons' mother, Miga´zi-Gan, had a sister named A´nman. If she was the A´nman who was the mother of Zachary and of Scott's wife, then Matthew and Nu´san Scott were "brother" and "sister" (parallel cousins). Also, the Larsons' mother would have been a cross-cousin of Cook (see Genealogy III). This connection has not been made on these genealogies because not verified.

Elders did not agree as to whether Aiyaq´saq (30D) was the son of Nana´pin or of ANatoa´paGakh.

III. One of Ernest Norton's grandmothers was named Awi´LiGan—

probably the one whom Christine called Bent Woman, but whether she was Taʹolan's mother or Paniʹsagakh's mother was not known (or not recorded).

The father of Matthew Larson's wife, Aʹgiyakh, was Momikhaʹ-Lagia; her mother was "Zachary's wife," but it was not certain whether his first or second wife. On available evidence, it is assumed that the latter, KaʹnnaGan, was her mother.

The Uyuʹkochiʹakh who was adopted by James probably was the brother of Martha whose name was not verified. He is so treated here.

IV. It is likely that the father of Paʹnchakan (Russell's first wife) was named MomikhaʹLagia.

Celia's father's name was not learned; but since she was said to be a half sister of Herbert *et al.*, her father must have been Chakiʹgakh. (She and Herbert had different mothers.)

The Nusaʹlaq (388E) who was a daughter of KaʹnnoaN and sister of Alberta may have been the Nusaʹlaq (388C) who married Aaron but is not so treated here for lack of evidence. If they were the same, then IlaGaʹLagia also would be a sister of Alberta, which is contraindicated.

VII. There is a question as to whether the third daughter of Lucinda was the child of her second husband, ManiʹGanakh, or third husband, Chris. There were conflicting statements as to whether Aguʹyelukhchoakh (27A), deceased, was the son of NaʹuwaGakh (369C) or Awiʹgiyakh (105E).

VIII. It is possible but not probable that the KiawiʹGakh (252A) who was Gregory's grandfather was the KiawiʹGakh (252B) who married Rachel and her mother.

Celia may have had another son who died, not shown here because so much in doubt.

It is probable and accepted here, although not verified, that the TachiʹLka who was Oliver's father was the TachiʹLka who was father of Zachary and Constance.

IX. Russell and Kusaʹuyakh (283A) were "brothers," that is, parallel cousins. UmGaʹGakh (514C) and Chaʹqa (135A) may have been sisters, or AʹpaGayakh (90A) and Kusaʹuyak's "unknown" father may have been brothers. The latter is more likely.

Possibly Ada's mother, NaʹugoGakh (370B), was a sister of Constance's father and Aunt ANaʹGakh, that is, Ada and Constance may have been "sisters," parallel cousins. This relationship would account for Ada's name, ANaʹGakh, and for Constance's adoption of Ada's son, Lars.

IX and X. The Ermiloffs should have been distinguished. There were two different Ermiloffs from the mainland, Russian-Eskimo and related to each other.

For other questions on relationships, see coded list of Eskimo names and identifications.

KEY TO GENEALOGIES

Personal Number	Eskimo Name	Identification, by Relationship	Occurrence, by Genealogy Number
3A	ačugu'nax	Son of Elizabeth	I, X
6A	a'ganači'ax	Sister of Amelia	V, VI
6B	a'ganači'ax	Louise, daughter of Rose	V, VII, VIII
6C	a'ganači'ax	Daughter of Wilson	VIII, X
7A	a'ganaču'Nax	Jane, wife of Matthew and Lewis	VI, X
7B	a'ganaču'Nax	Wife of Herbert, sister of Juliet	VII
7C	a'ganaču'Nax	Mother of Ralph Johnson and Dan Johnson	I, IX, X
7D	a'ganaču'Nax	Daughter of Ralph Johnson and Martha	X
7E	a'ganaču'Nax	Harriet, daughter of Ralph and Rose	VII, X
8A	a'ganaga'čuNax	Sister of Harmon, mother of Pearl	III
8B	a'ganaga'čuNax	Judy Cook, sister of Duncan	III, VI, IX
9A	a'ganaga'pax	(Called also ača'čax?) Half sister of i'NaN	III
9B	a'ganaga'pax	Claudia Field, sister of Raymond	III
10A	a'ganaGai'ax	Son of Andy	I, VIII
10B	a'ganaGai'ax	Daughter of u'mian	IV
10C	a'ganaGai'ax	Paternal grandfather of Daniel	V
10D	a'ganaGai'ax	Aunt of Alberta	IV
10E	a'ganaGai'ax	Dennis, father of Ethan	I, II
10F	a'ganaGai'ax	Father of Aaron	I
11A	a'gana'qčux (or -čix?)	Daughter of Rhoda and Theodore	V
12A	a'gana'kox (or a'ganao'kox?)	Catherine, wife of Victor	I, II, IV, VIII
13A	a'gana'mčux	Sister of Daniel	V
13B	a'gana'mčux	Second Mildred, daughter of Christine	III
14A	agana'tkan	Sister of Daniel	V
14B	agana'tkan	Anne, wife of Paul Scott	III, V, VI
14C	agana'tkan	Juliet, wife of Ethan	II, VII
15A	aganaya'Gax	Rosamond, wife of Ernest Norton	IX
20A	aGi'Gan	Wife of Harmon, sister of Lewis	III, X
21A	a'giyax	First wife of Matthew	III, VI
22A	a'giya'gax	Daughter of Chris Daniel	V
26A	agu'yəlux	Noah, son of Austin	V, VI, IX
26B	agu'yəlux	Simon, first husband of Ada	IX
27A	agu'yəluxčoax	Brother (or half brother?) of Rickie	VII
30A	aiya'qsaq	Son of Adam Larson	VI
30B	aiya'qsaq	Rob, son of Lucinda	VII, IX
30C	aiya'qsaq	Father of Amelia	V
30D	aiya'qsaq	Isaac, husband of Rose	II, III, VII, VIII
30E	aiya'qsaq	Father of ki'uGan	VIII
30F	aiya'qsaq	Son of lu'xtusi'ga	IX, X
35A	aka'łiNox	Husband of Constance	VIII
36A	a'qəqox	Son of Tim	VII

Personal Number	Eskimo Name	Identification, by Relationship	Occurrence, by Genealogy Number
37A	a'qoaq (or a'quaX ?)	Father of čani'aGa'łagia	I, V, X
37B	a'qoaq	Husband of Esther and Lillian	I, III, IV,VIII, X
41A	alali'kax	Alfred Cook, brother of Duncan	III, IX
41B	alali'kax	Father of Lewis	III, X
41C	alali'kax	Son of Esther	I, VII, VIII
46A	amu'kan	Daughter of Lucinda	VII
50A	anaGa'qa(x)	Leila, daughter of Paul Scott	III
50B	anaGa'qa(x)	(Called also ača'łux) Stepgrandmother of Gregory	VIII
51A	a'n. aGan	Mother of Jeffrey and Fred Matthew	VI, VII
51B	a'n. aGan	Daughter of Jeffrey	VI
52A	a'n. aGaN	Mother of Helene	I, V
53A	a'n. aGa'gax (or a'n. ago'gax?)	Daughter of Bob Wilson	VIII
53B	a'n. aGa'gax	Daughter of Victor, adopted by May	I, VI
60A	a'n. igi'lax	Son of Herbert, adopted by Lewis	VII, X
60B	a'n. igi'lax	Husband of nuyə'Gayux (also of pani'sagax?)	V, IX
60C	a'n. igi'lax	Son of Simon and Ada, adopted by Ernest	IX
61A	ani'yax	Wife of Billy and Tim	III, VII
65A	ə'n. mən	Rhoda, daughter of Helene	IV, V, VI
65B	ə'n. mən	Mother of Stephen (evidently not the same as Christine's grandmother)	V, VIII
65C	ə'n. mən	Mother of nu'sən, niece of Aaron, possibly sister of miga'ziGan	I, II, III, VIII
65D	ə'n. mən	Daughter of Zachary	VIII
68A	ano'nax	Daughter of ki'uGan	VIII
70A	aNa'Gax	Probably name of daughter of Mary Russell	III, IV
70B	aNa'Gax	Ada, wife of Luther	II, V, IX
70C	aNa'Gax	Daughter of Russell	III, IV
70D	aNa'Gax	First Mildred, daughter of Christine	III
70E	aNa'Gax	Mother of Gregory	II, VIII
70F	aNa'Gax	Mother of Russell's first wife	IV
71A	aNa'sax	Husband of Rachel (probably i'GinaXao'čin)	I
73A	aNatoa'paGax	Husband of Esther	I, VII, VIII
73B	aNatoa'paGax	Father of Edwin Larson	II, III, VI
74A	aNa'win	Mother or maternal aunt of Daniel (probably mother)	V
80A	aNi'lan	Wife of Aaron	I
81A	a'NinaQax	Husband of Sophie	VIII, IX
85A	aNu'tika'yax (or -kai'ax?)	Harmon, brother-in-law of Lewis	I, III, VII, X
86A	aNu'tiNeax	Dick (or Richard), son of Lewis	VI, X
90A	a'paGayax	Father of Scott	III, IV
90B	apɔa'γax	Fritz Russell, husband of May	IV, VIII
91A	apa'zu	Son-in-law of Russell (man from the mainland)	III, IV
92A	apu'Gan	Wife of Charlie Sharp	IV, VIII
92B	apu'Gan	Wife of u'mian	IV, VI

Personal Number	Eskimo Name	Identification, by Relationship	Occurrence, by Genealogy Number
92C	apu'Gan	Aunt of Paul Scott	III
96A	atakwi'łiNox	(Called also ka'yaxki'łiNox) Field, brother of aiya'qsaq	II, III
100A	aqsi'gax (or aXsi- ?)	Celia, half sister of Catherine, mother of ki'uGan	I, IV, VII, VIII, IX
105A	awi'giax	Brother of Harmon	III
105B	awi'giax	Son of Clarence	VI
105C	awi'giax	Duncan Cook, son-in-law of Daniel	III, V, IX
105D	awi'giax	Father of John and Clarence, also of i'NaN	II, III, VI
105E	awi'giax	Ethan, son of Dennis	II, IV, VII
105F	awi'giax	Father of James, evidently not same as father of John and Clarence	X
106A	awi'łaGan	Wife of čani'aGa'łagia	I, IV, X
106B	awi'łaGan	Grandmother of Ernest Norton (see Note)	III, V
106C	awi'łaGan	Daughter of a'NinaQax	IX
107A	awu'xta(x)	Daughter of Jeffrey and Dora	VI
111A	ayaGa'lagia	Wife of Edwin Larson and Richard Chappel's father	II, IV, IX
112A	aya'gaxtox	Grandson of kusau'yax	IV, IX
112B	aya'gaxtox	Son of kakia'nax	II, VI
113A	ayə'puan	Joe, son of Edwin Larson	I, II
114A	ayəGu'naq	Wife of Homer Larson (from the mainland)	III, VI
125A	ča'galox	Son of Herbert	VII
127A	čaga'v. alan (or čagə'v- ?)	Mary, daughter of Russell	III, IV
128A	čagi'Gan	Lucinda, sister of Herbert	II, IV, VII, VIII
129A	čagu'miXlux	Chris Daniel, husband of Esther and Judith	I, V, VII, VIII
135A	ča'qa	Aunt of Helene (same ča'qa as Scott's mother)	I, III, IV
135B	ča'qa	Esther, wife of Chris and a'qoaq	I, V, VII, VIII, X
135C	ča'qa	Daughter of Ethan	II
135D	ča'qa	Christine, wife of Gregory	III, VII
135E	ča'qa	Wife of Simon (same as Helene's aunt?)	IX
136A	čaka'Xax	Son of Simon and Ada	IX
137A	čaki'Gan	Son of Daniel	V
140A	čaki'Gax	Father of ka'kia'nax and Herbert (same as father of Celia?)	II, IV, VII, IX
140B	čaki'Gax	Probably name of father of Celia	VIII
141A	čaki'Gagax	Son of Ethan	II
142A	čaki'lax	Thomas, son of Paul Scott	III
143A	čaki'łax	Asael Sharp, husband of Alberta	IV
146A	čani'aGa'łagia	Adolph, adopted by Aaron	I, VIII, X
146B	čani'aGa'łagia	Father of apu'Gan and no'GaN	III, VI, VII, X
146C	čani'aGa'łagia	Joshua, nephew of Daniel	I, IV, V, VIII, X
146D	čani'aGa'łagia	Fred, son of Matthew	VI, X
146E	čani'aGa'łagia	Son of Herbert	VII
146F	čani'aGa'łagia	Son of Tim	VII

Personal Number	Eskimo Name	Identification, by Relationship	Occurrence, by Genealogy Number
146G	čaniʾaGaʾłagia	Steve, son of Ezra	VII
147A	čaniʾkoguyax	James, husband of paniʾnagax	VII, X
147B	čaniʾkoguyax	Arnold, stepson of Ralph Johnson	X
151A	čaʾXax	Jeffrey, son of Matthew	VI
151B	čaʾXax	Lillian, wife of kiʾuGan	VIII, X
151C	čaʾXax	Sister of Cook	IX
155A	čikaiʾyux	Judith, wife of Chris	II, V, VIII
156A	čikiʾyax	Son of Catherine	I, IV, VIII
157A	čikuʾłkaʾGax	(Also called načiʾxnax) Ernest Norton, son of paniʾsagax	III, IX, X
160A	čimiʾgax	Joel, son of John	III, VI
160B	čimiʾgax	Possibly name of son of Dick Lewis	X
161A	čixmeʾaGałagia	Wife of Alfred Daniel	IV, V, VII
161B	čixmeʾaGałagia	Mother of noʾGaN and aʾnaGan	VI, VII
161C	čixmeʾaGałagia	Daughter of Tim	VII
165A	čiNaiʾyaGan	Sister of Daniel	I, V, X
170A	čuʾqa	Husband of puʾgulaGaʾłagia	II, IV, V, VIII
170B	čuʾqa	Theodore, husband of Rhoda	IV, V
171A	čukaiʾyax (or -kaʾyax?)	Wife of kaʾkiaʾnax and Bernard	II, VI
171B	čukaiʾyax	Virginia, daughter of Solomon Cannon	VI, IX
171C	čukaiʾyax	Son of Tim	VII
172A	čukiʾliyaʾGax	Son of Isaac and Rose	VII
172B	čukiʾliyaʾGax	Benson, brother of aʾganačuʾNax	IX, X
173A	čukiʾyax	Uncle of Benson	X
176A	čuNaʾGax	Brother of Richard Chappel	III, IV
177A	čupuʾGaniʾaGałagia	Clarissa, wife of Ted Cook	IV, IX
181A	ičaʾganix	Mother of Rose	II, VII, IX
181B	ičaʾganix	Ellen, daughter-in-law of Russell	IV, VII
181C	ičaʾganix	(Also called ičaʾganin) Wife of Daniel (same as Ezra's mother?)	II, V
181D	ičaʾganix	Barbara, adopted by Jane Matthew	VI, VII
186A	igaʾlox	Brother of čuʾqa and paniʾsagax	V
186B	igaʾlox	Brother of Amelia	V
186C	igaʾlox	Son of Rachel	V
188A	iʾginaXaoʾčin	(Also called aNaʾsax) Father of Ezra	II, VII, IX
191A	ilaGaʾłagia	Mother of Elizabeth	I
195A	iluwaGaʾłagia	Austin, half brother of Rachel	I, V, VI, IX
195B	iluwaGaʾłagia	Brother of Daniel	V
198A	iʾm. in	Daughter of Ellen	IV
198B	iʾm. in	Sister of Juliet	VII
198C	iʾm. in	Son of Tim	VII
200A	inuʾtaN	Wife of Austin	V, VI, IX, X
200B	inuʾtaN	Child of Chris Daniel (sex unspecified, probably female)	V
200C	inuʾtaN	Adopted daughter of Zachary	VIII, IX
205A	iʾNaN	Grandfather of Christine	II, III, X
205B	iʾNaN	Son of maniʾGanax	VII
210A	ixčuNaiʾyax	Brother of Asael Sharp	II, IV, X
210B	ixčuNaiʾyax	Aunt (or uncle?) of Asael	IV
215A	ivaʾlu	Husband of Dorothy Gregory	III, IV

Personal Number	Eskimo Name	Identification, by Relationship	Occurrence, by Genealogy Number
220A	ka'kia'nax	Son of Lucinda	VII
220B	ka'kia'nax	Jimmie, son of Dennis	I, VII
220C	ka'kia'nax	Father of Dennis	II, X
220D	ka'kia'nax	Uncle of Herbert	II, VI, IX
221A	kako'xtax	Daughter of Juliet	VII
225A	kali'Gamiun	Paul Scott, brother of Christine	III, IV, VI
225B	kali'Gamiun	Brother of Scott and Russell	III, VI
228A	ka'n. aGan	Aunt of Stephen	V
228B	ka'n. aGan	Wife of Zachary	II, III, VII, VIII
229A	ka'n. aGa'Gan	Mother of Celia	IV, VIII
230A	ka'n. oaN	Father of Alberta	IV
230B	ka'n. oaN	Son of Asael Sharp and Alberta	IV
235A	ka'Nanax	Luther Norton, brother of Amelia	V, VI, IX
236A	ka'Nalix	Maternal uncle of the Larsons	II
236B	ka'Nalix	Bernard Larson, husband of May	I, II, VI, VIII
236C	ka'Nalix	Richard Chappel, husband of Jessie	IV, VIII
238A	kapu'Gan	Patrick, son of Clarence	VI, VIII
238B	kapu'Gan	Father of Richard Chappel	I, IV
240A	(see 288A)		
241A	kaowi'giax	(Nickname; real name forgotten) Father of Stephen	V, VIII
245A	kaya'Gax	Jerome, brother of Ernest	IX
248A	ka'zigi'a(x)	Husband of Lucinda	VII, VIII
248B	ka'zigi'a(x)	Son of Celia	VIII
248C	ka'zigi'a(x)	Louis, son of Asael Sharp	IV
249A	kazgai'ax (or ka'zigi'a?)	Mother of Alberta	IV
252A	kiawi'Gax (or keawi'Gax?)	Grandfather of Gregory and May	VIII
252B	kiawi'Gax	Father of Austin	I, V
252C	kiawi'Gax	Gregory, husband of Christine	I, III, VIII
255A	ki'Giwan	Son of Herbert	VII
258A	kima'GaGax	First wife of Adam Larson	VI, VII
258B	kima'GaGax	Possibly name of daughter of Esther	VII
258C	kima'GaGax	Son of Oliver	VIII
258D	kima'GaGax	(Also called mała'gax) Sophie, adopted daughter of Benson	V, VIII, X
258E	kima'GaGax	Daughter of Wilbert Daniel	V
260A	ki'nax	Daughter of Lewis, wife of Adolph	III, VIII, X
261A	ki'naxta'Gax	Father of patu'łagia	VI
261B	ki'naxta'Gax	Son of patu'łagia	VI
265A	kinu'Gan	Wife of Clarence	VI, VIII
265B	kinu'Gan	Granddaughter of Celia	VIII
268A	kiNwiaGa'łagia	Ezra, son of iča'ganix	II, VII, VIII, IX
270A	ki'uGan	Son of Celia	VII, VIII
270B	ki'uGan	Son of Adolph	VIII
270C	ki'uGan	Father of Asael Sharp	IV
270D	ki'uGan	Charlie, son of Asael Sharp	IV, VIII
271A	kiogoyu'Gax	Sammy, son of Bob Wilson and Sophie	V, VIII
271B	kiogoyu'Gax	Brother of Cook	I, VI, VIII, IX
275A	ki'ziNa'łagia	Mother of Lewis	III, X

Personal Number	Eskimo Name	Identification, by Relationship	Occurrence, by Genealogy Number
278A	koka'ɬagox (see 295C)	(Also called lagau'taGax) Mother of Asael Sharp	IV
279A	ko'nako'siN	Wife of Duncan Cook	V
279B	ko'nako'siN	Mother of Lydia	I, IV, V
279C	ko'nako'siN	Hannah, sister of Pearl, mother of Virginia (not same as Lydia's mother)	IX
282A	ko'guyax	Danny, son of Gregory	III
282B	ko'guyax	Maternal uncle of Daniel (possibly same as Gregory's father)	V, VIII
282C	ko'guyax	Grandson of čukai'yax	II, VI
283A	kusau'yax	Father of puyugone'gax	IV, VI, IX
283B	kusau'yax	Adam Larson, brother of Bernard	V, VI, IX
283C	kusau'yax	Father of Matthew	II, VI
286A	kuɬua'Qax	Daughter of Dan Johnson and Pearl	IX
287A	ku'malui'ɬiNox	Probable name of daughter of Fritz Russell	IV
287B	ku'malui'ɬiNox	Jessie, wife of Nicholas and Richard	I, IV
288A	kuNu'xkax (or kaNo'xkax?)	(Also called kao'wagax) Owen, son of Matthew	VI, IX
288B	kuNu'xkax	Son of Asael Sharp	IV
288C	kuNu'xkax	Cook, husband of Pearl	II, III, VI, IX, X
289A	kuNu'xtox	Solomon Cannon, husband of Celia	VIII, IX
295A	lagau'taGax	Emily, adopted daughter of Ernest Norton	VII, IX
295B	lagau'taGax	Wife of a'qoaq and Paul Scott	III, IV, X
295C	lagau'taGax (see 278A)	Mother of Asael Sharp	IV
298A	luxtusi'Ga(x)	Son-in-law of kusau'yax	II, V, IX
298B	luxtusi'Ga(x)	Son of Joel John and Judy Cook	VI
298C	luxtusi'Ga(x)	Son of Matthew	VI
298D	luxtusi'Ga(x)	Son of Simon and Ada	IX
298E	luxtusi'Ga(x)	Aaron, husband of aNi'lan	I, II
298F	luxtusi'Ga(x)	John, father of Joel	II, VI
298G	luxtusi'Ga(x)	Probably name of son of Paul Scott and Anne	III
298I	luxtusi'Ga(x)	Paternal uncle of Daniel	V
300A	ɬu'wagax	Rose, wife of Isaac and Ralph Johnson	III, V, VII, VIII, X
300B	ɬu'wagax	Louis, adopted son of Benson	IX
300C	ɬu'wagax	Father of Benson	II, X
300D	ɬu'wagax	Mother of aiya'qsaq	II, III
300E	ɬu'wagax	Daughter of Wilbert Daniel	V
302A	ma'čian	Pearl, mother of Duncan Cook	III, IV, IX
303A	maču'Nax	Wife of Simon	IX
308A	maɬa'	Lewis, father of Dick	III, VI, VII, IX, X
309A	maɬa'guin	Daughter of Jeffrey Matthew and Dora	VI
312A	ma'ɬkoax	Brother of ču'qa	V
315A	malu'gaya'Gan	Russell, brother of Scott	III, IV, VI
318A	ma'n.aq (or mə'n.aq?)	First wife of apa'zu	III

Personal Number	Eskimo Name	Identification, by Relationship	Occurrence, by Genealogy Number
318B	ma'n.aq	Daughter of Tim	VII
320A	mani'Gax	Son of Isaac and Rose	VII
320B	mani'Gax	Wife of Benson	X
321A	mani'Ganax	Brother of Martha	III, VII, X
325A	ma'soa'lox	Husband of ko'nako'siN	I
325B	ma'soa'lox	Hans, son of Lydia	I, VI, VIII
328A	miga'ziGan	Mother of the Larsons	II, VI
328B	miga'ziGan	Sister of ču'qa, wife of kusau'yax	V, IX
328C	miga'ziGan	Sister of Daniel	V
330A	miknai'yax	Daughter of Simon, adopted by Adam Larson	IX
331A	mi'yax	Daughter of Chris and Judith, adopted by Luther Norton	V
332A	miya'Gax	Martha, wife of Ralph Johnson	III, X
332B	miya'Gax	Gertrude, adopted daughter of Jane Matthew	III, V, VI, X
335A	momixka'łagia	Probably name of son of Ellen	IV
335B	momixka'łagia	Son of Russell	IV
335C	momixka'łagia	Father of Matthew's first wife	III
340A	nača'galux	Brother of Asael Sharp	I, IV
342A	nači'tnax	Son of Simon and Ada	IX
345A	nafe'aya'gax	Mother of Herbert	II, IV, VII
348A	naga'Xayax	Nicholas, husband of Lydia	I, IV, V, VIII
349A	nagaya'xtox	Daniel, husband of Amelia	I, II, V, VI, X
354A	nai'.Gax (or nai'yaGax?)	Alfred, son of Daniel	V, VII
354B	nai'.Gax	Probably name of son of Adam Larson	IX
354C	nai'.Gax	Matthew, father of Jeffrey	VI, IX
354D	nai'.Gax	Brother of Rachel	I, V
354E	nai'.Gax	Davy, son of Austin	I, V, IX
356A	na'qa (or na'ka)	Father of Rose	VII, VIII
356B	na'qa	Dan Johnson, husband of Pearl	IX, X
357A	nako'gutai'łiNox	Wife of Russell	IV, VI, VIII
360A	nana'pan	Father of aiya'qsaq	II, III
361A	nani'xkiun	Son of a'Ninaqax	VIII, IX
361B	nani'xkiun	Zachary, husband of ka'n.aGan	II, III, VIII
361C	nani'xkiun	Son of Paul Scott and Anne	III
364A	na'n.oq	(Also called ki'kitax) Scott, father of Christine	III
364B	na'n.oq	Son of Joel John	III, VI
364C	na'n.oq	Son of Paul Scott and Anne	III, X
365A	na'n.oxka'łagia	Wife of ču'qa	IV, VIII
368A	nao'Gax	Father of Bernard Larson	I, II, VI
369A	nao'wagax (or nau'aGax?)	Son of Adam Larson	VI
369B	nao'wagax	Son of Homer Larson	III, VI
369C	nao'wagax	Brother of Stephen	I, V, VII, VIII
370A	naoGo'Gax	Daughter of Simon	IX
370B	naoGo'Gax	Mother of ka'kia'nax	II, VII, IX
372A	naočia'Gax	Mother-in-law of Zachary	VIII
375A	na'v.agaun	Brother of Daniel	V
378A	nayə'Ganiq	Son of Jeffrey Matthew	VI

Personal Number	Eskimo Name	Identification, by Relationship	Occurrence, by Genealogy Number
378B	nayə'Ganiq	Wife of Ethan	II, IV
378C	nayə'Ganiq	Father of a'qoaq	III, X
381A	no'GaN	Wife of Clarence	VI, VII
381B	no'GaN	Rickie, son of Ethan	II, IV, VII
381C	no'GaN	Wife of Jack Dennis	I, VII
382A	noga'tax	Father of Solomon Cannon	IX
382B	noga'tax	Son of Solomon Cannon	IX
382C	noga'tax	Herbert, brother of Lucinda	II, III, IV, VII, IX
382D	noga'tax	Ted Cook, son of Pearl	III, IV, IX
383A	nogao'x	Lottie, daughter of Lydia	I
388A	nusa'l. aq	Wife of Lewis	III, VI, IX, X
388B	nusa'l. aq	Possibly name of daughter of Dick Lewis	X
388C	nusa'l. aq	Wife of Aaron	I
388D	nusa'l. aq	Daughter of Dennis and Elizabeth	I, VIII
388E	nusa'l. aq	Sister of Alberta (possibly same as 388C)	IV
389A	nu's. an	Daughter of Amelia and first husband (if he was tači'łka, then this nu's.an is Constance)	V
389B	nu's. an	Daughter of Jeffrey and Dora	VI
389C	nu's. an	Constance, wife of Ezra	III, VII, VIII
389D	nu's. an	(Also called ki'ziNa'łagia) Agnes, wife of Oliver	VIII, X
389E	nu's. an	Mother of Christine	III
389F	nu's. an	Dorothy, daughter of Christine	III
389G	nu's. an	Mother of a'qoaq	I, V, VI, X
389H	nu's. an	Daughter of Chris Daniel	IV, V
389I	nu's. an	Daughter of Dennis and Elizabeth	I, X
389J	nu's. an	Daughter of Bob Wilson	VIII
390A	nuyə'gayux	Step-mother and wife of Luther Norton	V, IX
392A	nuyə'łaGan	Betsy, wife of Wilbert Daniel	V, VII
395A	paču'Nia	May, wife of Bernard	I, VI, VIII
397A	pa'nčakan (or -Gan?)	Wife of Russell	III, IV
397B	pa'ncakan	Granddaughter of Russell	III, IV
400A	pani'gačuNax	Daughter of Scott	III, VI
400B	pani'gačuNax	Melissa, daughter of Paul Scott	III, IV
401A	pani'gaGax	Daughter of Dennis	I
401B	pani'gaGax	Grandmother of Dennis	II
401C	pani'gaGax	Sister of Dennis	II, III, IX, X
403A	pani'kapiax (or pani'Xpiax?)	Mother of čukai'yax	II
403B	pani'kapiax	Mother of Simon	IX
406A	pani'naGax	Daughter of Chris Daniel and Judith	V
406B	pani'naGax	Wife of Edwin Larson	II
406C	pani'naGax	Wife of James (possibly same as 406B)	X
408A	pani'Na'łaGan	Daughter of Alfred Cook	V, VII
410A	pani'saGax	Mother of Ernest Norton	III, IV, V, IX
412A	pani'xqax (-kax)	Sister of Herbert	II, IV, VII

Personal Number	Eskimo Name	Identification, by Relationship	Occurrence, by Genealogy Number
412B	pani′xqax	Grandmother of Gregory	II, VII, VIII
413A	pani′xkiun	(Also called ali′katax) Kate, wife of Jimmie Dennis	I, II, V, VIII
413B	pani′xkiun	Amelia, wife of Daniel	V, VI
413C	pani′xkiun	Marjory, daughter of Lewis	IX, X
417A	pantu′Nan	Elizabeth, wife of Dennis	I, II, III
417B	pantu′Nan	Mother of Luther Norton	V, IX
420A	patu′łagia	Wife of John, mother of Joel	III, V, VI
420B	patu′łagia	Daughter of Joel John	III, VI, X
420C	patu′łagia	Daughter of Herbert	VII
424A	pau′gu′łagia	Ralph Johnson, husband of Rose	I, VII, X
425A	pau′goyux	Son of Daniel, husband of Anne	III, V, VI
425B	pau′goyux	Brother of Daniel	V
425C	pau′goyux	Possibly name of son of Chris Daniel	V
430A	piNai′yan	Brother of John	VI
434A	pu′gulaGa′łagia	Wife of Aaron and tači′łka	I, II, IV, VIII, IX
435A	puguya′xtox	Clarence, half-brother of John	II, V, VI, VIII
438A	pu′psux	Paternal uncle of Ernest Norton	III
440A	pu′tu	Son of u′mian, nephew of Bernard	IV
440B	pu′tu	Brother of Bernard Larson	II
440C	pu′tu	Son of Adam Larson	IX
443A	puxtau′gox	Husband of Daniel's aunt?	V
443B	puxtau′gox	Son of Adam Larson	IX
446A	puyu′gonix	Mother of Dennis	II, V, X
446B	puyu′gonix	Sister of kusau′yax, possibly mother of patu′łagia	VI, IX
447A	puyugoni′Gax	Probably name of great-grand-daughter of kusau′yax	IV
447B	puyugoni′Gax	Daughter of kusau′yax	VI, IX
451A	tači′łka	Husband of a′n.man	II, III, VIII
451B	tači′łka	Gilbert, son of Gregory	III
451C	tači′łka	Son of Oliver	VIII
455A	tagu′łagia	Son of Victor	I, II
458A	talaGa′łagia	Son of Rose	VII
460A	tała′łagia	Alberta, wife of Asael Sharp	IV
463A	tałi′lix	Husband of Rachel, father of Arthur	I, V
463B	tałi′lix	Norbert, son of Lydia	I
464A	tałi′xtox	(Also called nayə′ganiq) Helene, mother of Rhoda	I, V, VI, VIII
466A	tana′Gax	Grandfather of Dennis	II
468A	ta′n.agix	Husband of ko′nako′siN	I, V, VIII, X
468B	ta′n.agix	Victor, son of Elizabeth	I, II, VIII
468C	ta′n.agix	Probably name of son of Gregory	I
468D	ta′n.agix	Stephen, husband of Helene	V, VI, VIII
468E	ta′n.agix	Son of Theodore and Rhoda	V
470A	ta′n.aka′łagia	Lydia, daughter of ta′n.agix	I, V, VIII
470B	ta′n.aka′łagia	Jack, son of Dennis	I, VII
474A	tao′lan	Father of Ernest Norton	III, V, IX
474B	tao′lan	Brother of Stephen	V, VIII, IX
477A	tixki′łiNox	Edwin Larson, father of Joe	II, VI, IX
477B	tixki′łiNox	Raymond, nephew of nu′san Scott	III, VI
480A	tu′čian	Maternal uncle of Daniel	V

Personal Number	Eskimo Name	Identification, by Relationship	Occurrence, by Genealogy Number
484A	tuku'małagia	Marian, wife of tao'lan, adopted daughter of Benson	V, VI, IX, X
484B	tuku'małagia	Mother of Benson	II, X
486A	tumaGani'Gałagia	Sister of Ernest and Jerome Norton	IX
488A	tu'n. aga'lix	Brother of Richard Chappel	IV
490A	tu'ntux	Brother of Ernest and Jerome Norton	IX
492A	tuNu'yałagia	Arthur, son of Rachel	I, V
495A	tu'tkix	Wilbert, son of Daniel	V, VII
498A	tutu'mə'n	Tim, husband of ani'yax	III, VII, X
498B	tutu'mə'n	Paternal uncle of Daniel	V
501A	tuyu'Gan	Lars, son of Simon, adopted by Ezra	VII, VIII, IX
505A	ugu'yuGa'łagia	Sister of Daniel	V
506A	uku'yaGax (or ugu'yaGax?)	Mother of Solomon Cannon	IX
510A	u'luGan (or u'la-?)	Oliver, husband of Agnes	II, VIII, X
514A	umGa'Gax	Mother of Bernard, sister of Matthew	I, II, VI; VII
514B	umGa'Gax	Debby, daughter of Adam Larson	III, VI
514C	umGa'Gax	Mother of kusau'yax, possibly wife of upa'Gowax, possibly maternal grandmother of Cook and patu'łagia	III, IV, VI, IX
514D	umGa'Gax	Paternal grandmother of Matthew	VI
516A	u'mian	Son of Asael Sharp	II, IV
516B	u'mian	Father of Amelia	V, IX
516C	u'mian	Harold, son of Anne	III, VI
516D	u'mian	Father of Catherine	VIII
516E	u'mian	Son of Wilbert Daniel	V
520A	uNala'kčian (or uNu-?)	Billy, husband of Rose	V, VII, VIII, X
521A	uNuwi'aGa'łagia	Andy, husband of nusa'laq	I, VIII
522A	uNu'yaGa'łagia (cf. 505A)	Uncle of Daniel	V
525A	upa'Gowax (or upə'-?)	Brother of Aaron, father of Cook	I, III, VI, IX
530A	uqai'ix	Daughter of kusau'yax	VII, IX
531A	u(x)ka'łagia (or uqa'-?)	Homer, brother of Bernard	III, VI
534A	uya'lix	Uncle of Daniel?	V
535A	uya'Nli	Brother of Aaron	I, II, VIII
538A	uyuXoči'ax	Daughter of Richard Chappel and Jessie	IV
538B	uyuXoči'ax	Bob Wilson, husband of Sophie	V, VIII
538C	uyuXoči'ax	Adopted son of James, probably brother of Martha	III, X
541A	yuvagaGa'łagia	Rachel, half sister of Helene	I, IV, V
544A	yu'n. ax	Son of Jeffrey and Dora	VI

SYMBOLS USED IN NUNIVAK GENEALOGIES

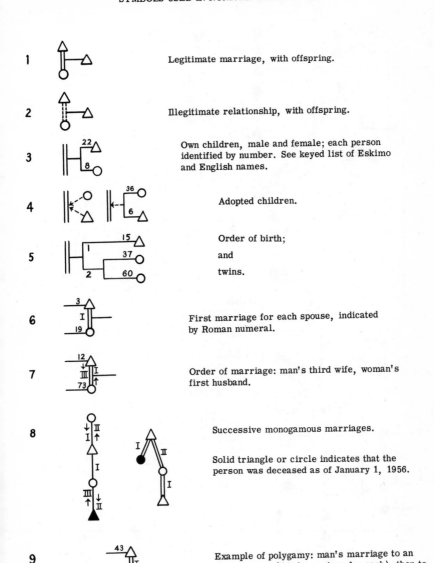

1. Legitimate marriage, with offspring.

2. Illegitimate relationship, with offspring.

3. Own children, male and female; each person identified by number. See keyed list of Eskimo and English names.

4. Adopted children.

5. Order of birth; and twins.

6. First marriage for each spouse, indicated by Roman numeral.

7. Order of marriage: man's third wife, woman's first husband.

8. Successive monogamous marriages.

Solid triangle or circle indicates that the person was deceased as of January 1, 1956.

9. Example of polygamy: man's marriage to an older woman (third marriage for each), then to a girl.

I

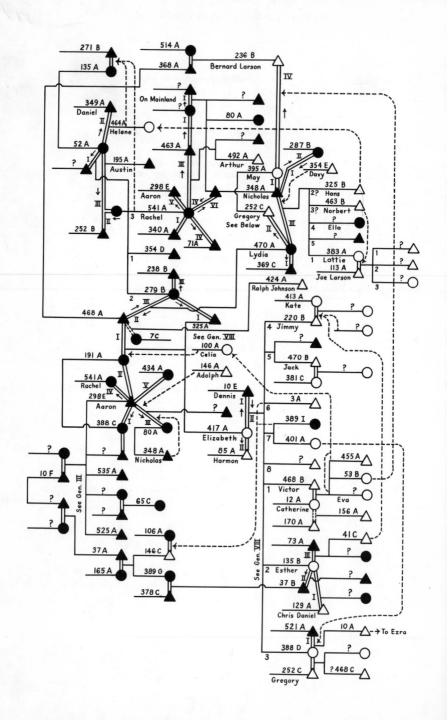

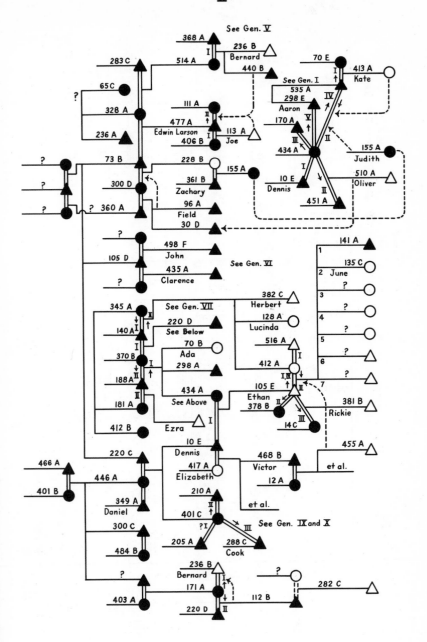

III

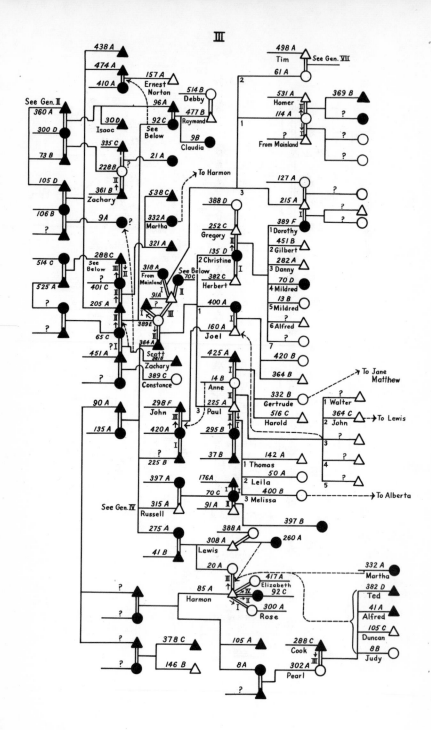

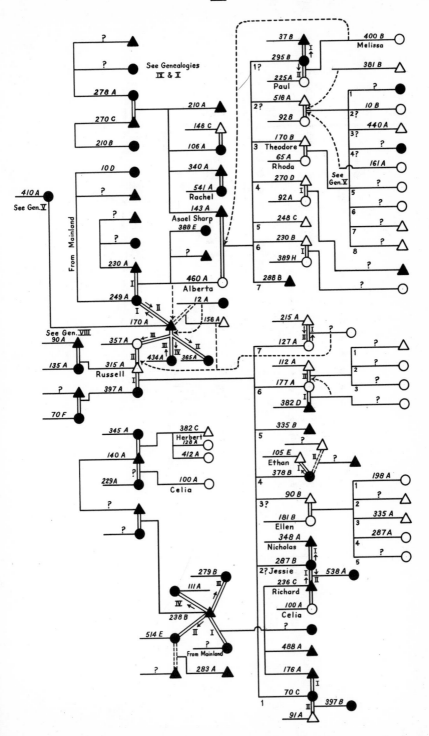

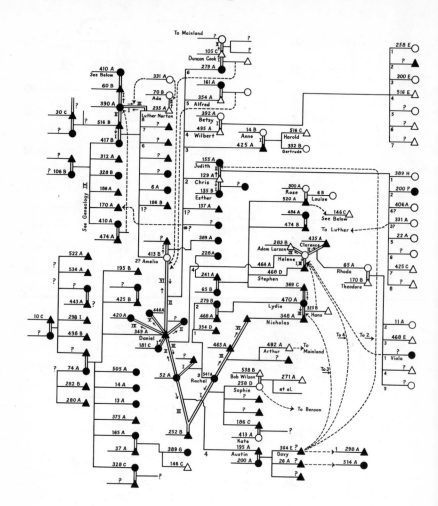

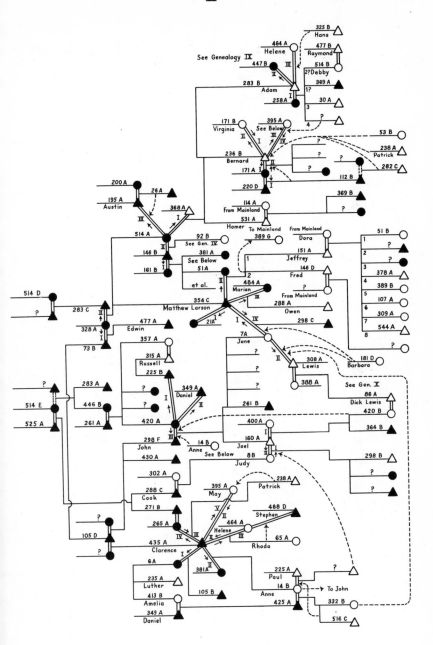

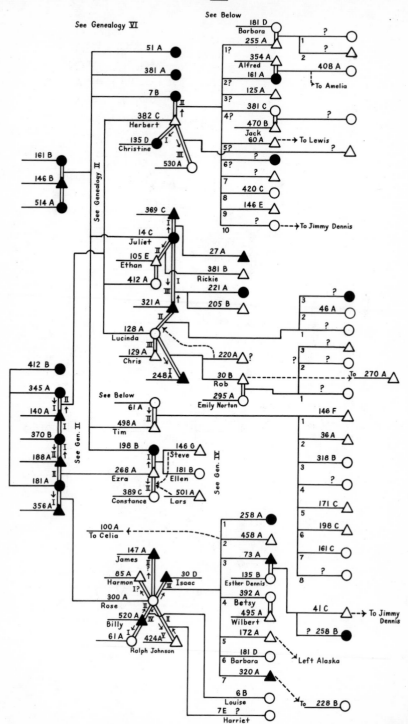

See Below

See Genealogy VI

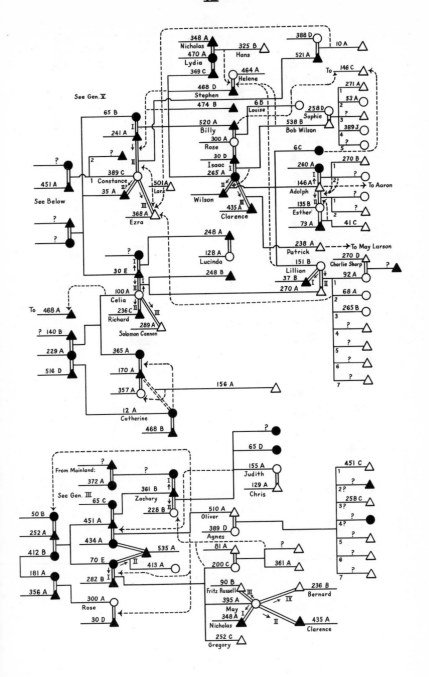

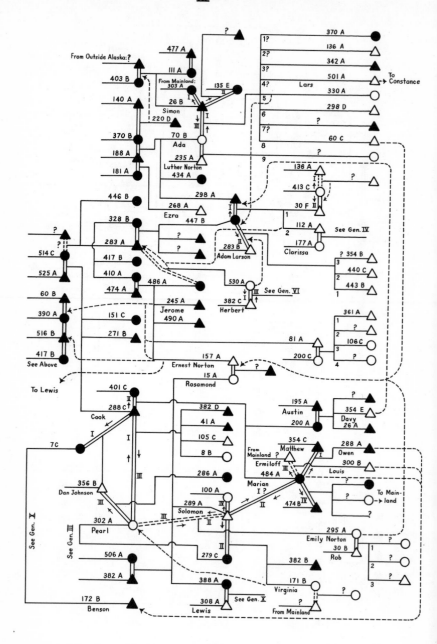

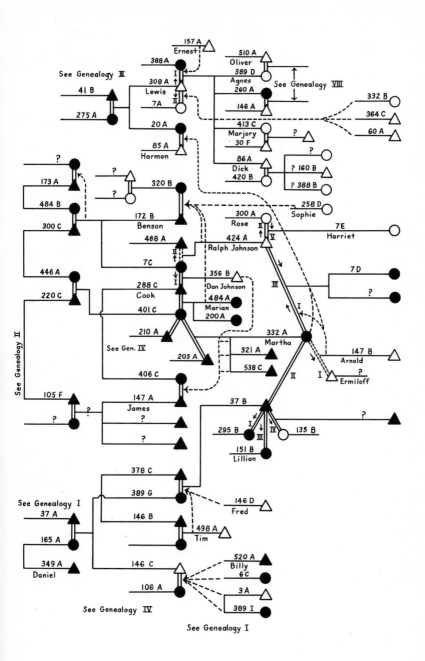

BIBLIOGRAPHY

Himmelheber, Hans. 1938. *Eskimokünstler*. Stuttgart: Strecker und Schröder.

———. 1951. *Der gefrorene Pfad*. Eisenach: Eric Röth.

Lantis, Margaret. 1946. The Social Culture of the Nunivak Eskimo. Philadelphia: Transactions of the American Philosophical Society, New Series, Vol. 35, Part III.

———. 1947. Alaskan Eskimo Ceremonialism. New York: American Ethnological Society, Monograph 11.

———. 1950. The Religion of the Eskimos. Forgotten Religions, V. Ferm (ed.). pp. 311-39. New York: Philosophical Library.

———. 1953. Nunivak Eskimo Personality as Revealed in the Mythology. Fairbanks: Anthropological Papers of the University of Alaska, 2:109-74.

———. 1959. Alaskan Eskimo Cultural Values. Polar Notes, No. 1, pp. 35-48. Hanover, N. H. : Dartmouth College Library.

Reiman, M. Gertrude. 1950. The Mosaic Test: Its Applicability and Validity. New York: American Journal of Orthopsychiatry, 20:600-15.

Only items presenting Nunivak source materials and data have been included.